ℒENT *and* ℰASTER ⱲISDOM
—— *from* ——
SAINT THÉRÈSE OF LISIEUX

Daily Scripture and Prayers Together
With Saint Thérèse of Lisieux's Own Words

John Cleary

Liguori
LIGUORI, MISSOURI

For my parents, John and Carol Cleary

~

Imprimi Potest: Stephen Rehrauer, CSsR, Provincial, Denver Province
The Redemptorists

Published by Liguori Publications, Liguori, Missouri 63057

To order, visit Liguori.org or call 800-325-9521.

Library of Congress Cataloging-in-Publication Data

Lent and Easter wisdom from Saint Thérèse of Lisieux / John Cleary— 1st ed.
   p. cm.

1. Lent—Prayers and devotions. 2. Easter—Prayers and devotions. 3. Catholic Church—Prayers and devotions. 4. Thérèse, de Lisieux, Saint, 1873–1897—Quotations. I. Title. II. Title: Lent and Easter wisdom from St. Thérèse of Lisieux.
BX2170.L4C54 2014
242'.34—dc23

2014031319

p ISBN: 978-0-7648-2173-8
e ISBN: 978-0-7648-6996-9

Quotations at the start of each chapter are from the Project Gutenberg ebook of *The Story of a Soul (L'Histoire d'une Âme): The Autobiography of St. Thérèse of Lisieux* by Thérèse Martin (of Lisieux). Translator: Thomas Taylor

Liguori Publications, a nonprofit corporation, is an apostolate of the Redemptorists. To learn more about the Redemptorists, visit Redemptorists.com.

Printed in the United States of America
First edition
19 18 17 16 15 / 5 4 3 2 1

Contents

Preface: A Path for Lent and Easter:
Thérèse's "Little Way"
~ iv ~

St. Thérèse of Lisieux: A Chronology
~ vi ~

Introduction
~ vii ~

PART I
Readings for Lent
~ 1 ~

PART II
Readings for Easter
~ 107 ~

Preface

A Path for Lent and Easter: Thérèse's "Little Way"

Thérèse Martin was born in Alençon, France, on January 2, 1873. Two days later, she was baptized Marie Frances Thérèse at Notre Dame Church to Louis Martin and Zélie Guérin. After her mother's death on August 28, 1877, Thérèse and her family moved to Lisieux.

On April 9, 1888, Thérèse entered the Carmel of Lisieux. She received the habit on the next January 10 and made her religious profession on September 8, 1890, on the feast of the Birth of the Blessed Virgin Mary.

In Carmel she embraced the way of perfection outlined by the foundress, St. Teresa of Jesus, fulfilling with genuine fervor and fidelity the various responsibilities entrusted to her. Her faith was tested by the sickness of her beloved father, Louis Martin, who died on July 29, 1894. Thérèse nevertheless grew in sanctity, enlightened by the word of God and inspired by the Gospel to place love at the center of everything. In her autobiographical writings, she left her recollections of childhood and adolescence and a portrait of her soul, the description of her most intimate experiences. She discovered the "little way" of spiritual childhood and taught it to the novices entrusted to her care. Seized by the love of Christ, she became increasingly aware of her apostolic and missionary vocation to draw everyone in her path toward that one love as well.

Her time of trial continued as her health declined, but new graces led her to perfection, and she discovered fresh insights for the diffusion of her message in the Church. Thérèse accepted her sufferings and trials with patience up to the moment of her death on the afternoon of September 30, 1897. Her final words were: "My God, I love you." This simple statement sealed a life that was extinguished at twenty-four. Soon a new phase of apostolic presence on behalf of the souls in the communion of saints was begun, as Thérèse had desired, in order to shower a rain of roses upon the world.

Thérèse was canonized by Pope Pius XI on May 17, 1925.

Both her teachings and example of holiness have been received with great enthusiasm by all sectors of the faithful ever since, as well as by people outside the Catholic Church and outside Christianity.

In view of the soundness of her spiritual wisdom inspired by the Gospel, the originality of her theological intuitions filled with sublime teaching, and the universal acceptance of her spiritual message—which has spread through the translation of her works into more than fifty languages—Pope John Paul II proclaimed Thérèse of the Child Jesus a doctor of the Church on World Mission Sunday, October 19, 1997. This is an honor the Catholic Church confers upon a person who has led a notably holy life and helped the propagation of Christian values and thoughts.

St. Thérèse of Lisieux: Made by God, for God. While this truth may be lost on us, it was never lost on "The Little Flower." She is a great saint, a precious woman who realized her "littleness" to such a degree that she understood the more she made herself small the closer the Lord would draw her near. In her "little way," Thérèse found the presence of the Lord in the tiniest facets of his creation, in every corner of her experience, in every little thing she said or did. God in all things, indeed! God gave Thérèse everything she had and, in turn, she made it her life's mission to give everything back to him. Made by God, for God.

Throughout this Lenten and Easter journey, we will explore the wellspring that is the spirituality of St. Thérèse of Lisieux, one of the most beloved saints in the long history of the Catholic Church. May her "little way" to the Lord serve as our own path to a greater nearness and devotion to our Savior, and may our loving Jesus draw us closer to him as we contemplate his own sojourn toward death and resurrection. Know also that your spiritual growth and welfare is committed to my own prayers as you proceed along this worthy Lenten and Easter journey.

John Cleary
St. Louis, 2015

St. Thérèse of Lisieux

A CHRONOLOGY

1873 • On January 2, Thérèse Martin is born in Alençon, France, to Louis Martin and Zélie Guérin Martin. Two days later, she is baptized Marie Frances Thérèse at Notre Dame Church.

1877 • After the death of her mother on August 28, Thérèse and her family move to Lisieux.

1888 • On the feast of the Annunciation, Thérèse enters the Carmelite convent of Lisieux as a postulant.

1890 • Thérèse makes her profession on the feast of Our Lady's Nativity and, several weeks later, takes the veil.

1894 • Louis Martin dies in July.

1896 • Thérèse finishes writing her autobiography, *The Story of a Soul*, and gives it the prioress, who had ordered her to write her memoirs. Later that year, Thérèse begins coughing up blood and experiences spiritual depression.

1897 • Thérèse becomes seriously ill in April; in July she is taken to the convent infirmary and receives the last sacraments. On September 30, after much suffering, Thérèse dies, surrounded by her community.

1923 • Thérèse is beatified by Pope Pius XI.

1925 • Thérèse of the Child Jesus is canonized by Pope Pius XI on May 17.

1927 • Pope Pius XI names Thérèse Patroness of all Missionaries, together with St. Francis Xavier.

1980 • Pope John Paul II makes a pilgrimage to Lisieux.

1997 • Pope John Paul II proclaims St. Thérèse of Lisieux a doctor of the Church on October 19.

Introduction

MOST CATHOLICS SEEM TO BE AWARE of the forty-day period before the feast of Easter. Lent, which comes from the Anglo-Saxon word lencten, meaning "spring," is a time marked by particular rituals, such as the reception of ashes on Ash Wednesday or the decision to "give up French fries" as a Lenten practice. Is Lent broader than just these practices which seem to be left over from another era?

A BRIEF HISTORY OF LENT

IN THE FIRST THREE CENTURIES of the Christian experience, preparation for the Easter feast usually covered a period of one or two days, perhaps a week at the most. Saint Irenaeus of Lyons even speaks of a forty-hour preparation for Easter.

The first reference to Lent as a period of forty days' preparation occurs in the teachings of the First Council of Nicaea in AD 325 and, by the end of the fourth century, a Lenten period of forty days was established and accepted.

In its early development, Lent quickly became associated with the sacrament of baptism, since Easter was the great baptismal feast. Those who were preparing to be baptized participated in the season of Lent in preparation for the reception of the sacrament of baptism. Eventually, those who were already baptized considered it important to join those candidates preparing for baptism in their preparations for Easter. The customs and practices of Lent as we know them today soon took hold.

LENT AS A JOURNEY

LENT IS OFTEN PORTRAYED AS A JOURNEY, from one point in time to another point in time. The concept of journey is obvious for those experiencing the Rite of Christian Initiation of Adults (RCIA), the program of baptismal preparation conducted in most parishes during the season of Lent.

But Lenten preparation is not limited to those who are preparing to be baptized and join the Church.

For many Catholics, Lent is a journey that is measured from Ash Wednesday through Easter Sunday, but, more accurately, Lent is measured from Ash Wednesday to the beginning of the period of time known as the Triduum. Triduum begins after the Mass on Holy Thursday, continues through Good Friday, and concludes with the Easter Vigil on Holy Saturday. Lent officially ends with the proclamation of the Exsultet, "Rejoice O Heavenly Powers," during the Mass of Holy Saturday.

The Lenten journey is also a process of spiritual growth and, as such, presumes movement from one state of being to another state. For example, some people may find themselves troubled and anxious at the beginning of Lent as a result of a life choice or an unanswered question, and, at the end of Lent, they may fully expect a sense of conversion, a sense of peace, or perhaps simply understanding and acceptance. In this sense, Lent is a movement from one point of view to another or, perhaps, from one interpretation of life to a different interpretation. By whatever yardstick the journey is measured, it is not only the period of time that is important but the essential experiences of the journey that are necessary for a full appreciation of what is being celebrated.

PENITENTIAL NATURE OF LENT

A POPULAR UNDERSTANDING OF LENT is that it is a penitential period of time during which people attempt to become more sensitive to the role of sin in their lives. Lenten sermons will speak of personal sin, coming to an awareness of the sins of others and the effect such sin might have, and, finally, the sin that can be found within our larger society and culture. Awareness of sin, however, is balanced by an emphasis on the love and acceptance that God still has for humanity, despite the sinful condition in which we still find ourselves.

This awareness of sin and the need for penance is emphasized through the practice of meditation on the passion of the Lord, his suffering, and his death. There is also a traditional concern for the reception of the sacrament of reconciliation during Lent. Originally, the sacrament of reconciliation was celebrated before Lent began, the penance imposed on Ash Wednesday, and the prescribed penance was performed during the entire forty-day period.

Scripture, psalms, prayers, rituals, practices, and penance are the components of the Lenten journey. Each component, tried and tested by years of tradition, is one of the "engines" that drives the season and which brings the weary traveler to the joys of Easter.

SUMMONS TO PENITENTIAL LIVING

"JESUS CAME TO GALILEE, proclaiming the good news of God, and saying, 'The time is fulfilled, and the kingdom of God has come near; repent, and believe in the good news'" (Mark 1:14–15). This call to conversion announces the solemn opening of Lent. Participants are marked with ashes, and the words, "Repent, and believe in the good news," are prayed. This blessing is understood as a personal acceptance of the desire to take on the life of penance for the sake of the gospel.

The example of Jesus in the desert for forty days—a time during which he fasted and prayed—is imitated. It is time to center attention on conversion. During Lent, the expectation is to examine our lives and, through the practice of prayer, fasting, and works of charity, seek to conform our lives to Christ's. For some, this conversion will be a turning from sin to grace. For others, it will be a gracious turning toward the mystery of God in Christ. Whatever the pattern chosen by a particular pilgrim for an observance of Lent, it is hoped that this book will provide a useful support in the effort.

PART I

~~~~~

READINGS *for* LENT

DAY 1

The Little Way: Our Journey Begins

*G*od would not inspire desires which could not be realized, and that I may aspire to sanctity in spite of my littleness. For me to become great is impossible. I must bear with myself and my many imperfections; but I will seek out a means of getting to Heaven by a little way—very short and very straight, a little way that is wholly new. We live in an age of inventions; nowadays the rich need not trouble to climb the stairs, they have lifts instead. Well, I mean to try and find a lift by which I may be raised unto God, for I am too tiny to climb the steep stairway of perfection....

Thine Arms, then, O Jesus, are the lift which must raise me up even unto Heaven. To get there I need not grow; on the contrary, I must remain little, I must become still less.

THE STORY OF A SOUL, IX, "THE NIGHT OF THE SOUL"

SCRIPTURE

People were bringing children to him that he might touch them, but the disciples rebuked them. When Jesus saw this he became indignant and said to them, "Let the children come to me; do not prevent them, for the kingdom of God belongs to such as these. Amen, I say to you, whoever does not accept the kingdom of God like a child will not enter it." Then he embraced them and blessed them, placing his hands on them.

MARK 10:13–16

PRAYER

Lord, though I am too small to reach you by my own means, still I reach out to you. Hold me close to you, as a father would his child, and may your love fulfill my desire to love you as you ask that I love you. Without you, I am left to my imperfections and the sad despair that what I have is not enough to satisfy my needs. Lift me up, loving Father, and grant me what I need to be always near you so I might fulfill your command to love you with all that you provide me in my humility. Amen.

LENTEN ACTION

In what ways do your imperfections and weaknesses move you to rely more and more on the love of God? How has this reliance on the Lord grown as you've aged? Does this perspective move you to greater forgiveness of yourself? In what ways? In your reflections throughout Ash Wednesday, consider how Jesus draws you closer to him when you "make yourself small" and confess your inability to give him all that he asks of you by your will alone. Understand that it is your weakness that allows him to love you to the depths both you and he desire. Reflect on this "little way" to God. How does it suit you?

DAY 2

The Word of God Is Manna From Heaven

*H*owever beautiful and touching a book may be, my heart does not respond, and I read without understanding, or, if I understand, I cannot meditate. In my helplessness the Holy Scriptures... in them I find a hidden manna, genuine and pure. But it is from the Gospels that I find most help in the time of prayer; from them I draw all that I need for my poor soul. I am always discovering in them new lights and hidden mysterious meanings. I know and I have experienced that "the Kingdom of God is within us" (Luke 17:21). Our Lord has no need of books or teachers to instruct our souls. He, the Teacher of Teachers, instructs us without any noise of words.

THE STORY OF A SOUL, VIII, "PROFESSION OF SOEUR THÉRÈSE"

SCRIPTURE

The grass withers, the flower wilts, but the word of our God stands forever.

ISAIAH 40:8

Heaven and earth will pass away, but my words will not pass away.

MATTHEW 24:35

PRAYER

Oh Lord our God, Word made flesh, nourish and inspire me through your holy Scripture. It is your word that sustains me when I stumble and fall, it lifts me up when I am overcome by sadness, and it settles my mind when I am filled with worry. I ask that you move me to turn to your word each day, and that I share its inspiration with all people I meet throughout the day, that they may know your love and wisdom through me, in my own words and in my actions. Amen.

LENTEN ACTION

Make daily and/or nightly reading of the Gospels part of your Lenten spiritual routine for growth. Imagine yourself in scenes from the Gospel watching Jesus interact with those he encounters. For example: Select Luke 10:38–42. Imagine yourself a friend and a fellow villager of Mary, Martha, or Lazarus. You happen to meet one of them in the village and you are told that Jesus is coming to visit in Bethany. You express your interest to meet Jesus and through your friends find yourself invited to a dinner with them and Jesus. Close your eyes and try to imagine what your meeting and ensuing conversation with Jesus would be like. Draw some practical fruit from it.

DAY 3

FRIDAY AFTER ASH WEDNESDAY

Have Confidence in the Father's Infinite Mercy

O Jesus! Would that I could tell all little souls of Thine ineffable condescension! I feel that if by any possibility Thou couldst find one weaker than my own, Thou wouldst take delight in loading her with still greater favours, provided that she abandoned herself with entire confidence to Thine Infinite Mercy.

But, O my Spouse, why these desires of mine to make known the secrets of Thy Love? Is it not Thyself alone Who hast taught them to me, and canst Thou not unveil them to others? Yea! I know it, and this I implore Thee! I entreat Thee to let Thy Divine Eyes rest upon a vast number of little souls, I entreat Thee to choose, in this world, a legion of little victims of Thy love.

THE STORY OF A SOUL, XI, "A CANTICLE OF LOVE"

SCRIPTURE

I shall get up and go to my father and I shall say to him, "Father, I have sinned against heaven and against you. I no longer deserve to be called your son; treat me as you would treat one of your hired workers." So he got up and went back to his father. While he was still a long way off, his father caught sight of him, and was filled with compassion. He ran to his son, embraced him and kissed him. His son said to him, "Father, I have sinned against heaven and against you; I no longer deserve to be called your son." But his father ordered his servants, "Quickly bring the finest robe and put it on him; put a ring on his finger and sandals on his feet. Take the fattened calf and slaughter it. Then let us celebrate with a feast, because this son of mine was dead, and has come to life again; he was lost, and has been found." Then the celebration began.

LUKE 15:18–24

PRAYER

Good and generous Father, knowing your mercy is unconditional escapes me when I stray from you. May I know this great comfort and turn from my misery and return to your loving embrace. May I practice mercy toward those who have harmed me and unchain from my heart those feelings of anger, vengeance, and ill will that bind me and prevent me from loving as I am called to love. I ask this through your merciful Son and my loving Lord, Jesus Christ. Amen.

LENTEN ACTION

"Blessed are the merciful, for they will receive mercy" (Matthew 5:7). Can I be as generous with my mercy as I have known such generous mercy from my God? By God's grace, I will reach out to someone today with mercy and let that person know I am praying for each of us that mercy and forgiveness will be shared between us. I will make the first step, the most difficult and vulnerable step, for it is God who seeks to share his infinite mercy with his sons and daughters.

DAY 4

Our Childlike Cries Stir God's Loving Response

God's Love is made manifest as well in a simple soul which does not resist His grace as in one more highly endowed. In fact, the characteristic of love being self-abasement, if all souls resembled the holy Doctors who have illuminated the Church, it seems that God in coming to them would not stoop low enough. But He has created the little child, who knows nothing and can but utter feeble cries, and the poor savage who has only the natural law to guide him, and it is to their hearts that He deigns to stoop. These are the field flowers whose simplicity charms Him; and by His condescension to them Our Saviour shows His infinite greatness. As the sun shines both on the cedar and on the floweret, so the Divine Sun illumines every soul, great and small, and all correspond to His care—just as in nature the seasons are so disposed that on the appointed day the humblest daisy shall unfold its petals.

THE STORY OF A SOUL, I, "EARLIEST MEMORIES"

SCRIPTURE

I love the LORD, who listened
to my voice in supplication,
Who turned an ear to me
on the day I called.
I was caught by the cords of death;
the snares of Sheol had seized me;
I felt agony and dread.
Then I called on the name of the LORD,
"O LORD, save my life!"
Gracious is the LORD and righteous;
yes, our God is merciful.
The LORD protects the simple;
I was helpless, but he saved me.

PSALM 116:1–6

PRAYER

Oh Lord, my God, hear my cries! I have relied only on myself and I find myself wounded with sin and fault. You are the way to salvation, the bedrock foundation upon whom I must build my home. All other recourse is folly. Draw me near, oh Lord, I implore you. May I only rely on you for all the days of my life. I beg you, Lord, bend down to lift me up for I am as low and as small as I can be. Only you can answer my call. Hear my voice and raise me up to your bosom.

LENTEN ACTION

Who do I know who has fallen? Who do I know who has been outcast from my group? From my parish? From their own family? Can I hear their voice? I am called to include the excluded, but how difficult it is to reach out to them! Difficult for me, but never for the Lord. May the Lord move me in this direction and may he reach out to the outcast *through* me. Then it is God acting through me, his blessed tool. Open me to this possibility; may God direct it to a specific person I know. This is my calling for today.

DAY 5

FIRST SUNDAY OF LENT

I Find Comfort in the Lord My God

*A*t that time [during a particularly difficult period in the spiritual life of Thérèse] I had all kinds of interior trials which I found it impossible to explain to anyone; suddenly, I was able to lay open my whole soul. The Father [a priest who led the retreat Thérèse was attending] understood me in a marvelous way; he seemed to divine my state and launched me full sail upon that ocean of confidence and love in which I had longed to advance but so far had not dared. He told me that my faults did not pain the Good God and added: "At this moment I hold His place, and I assure you from Him that He is well-pleased with your soul."

How happy these consoling words made me! I had never been told before that it was possible for faults not to pain the Sacred Heart; this assurance filled me with joy and helped me to bear with patience the exile of this life.

THE STORY OF A SOUL, VIII, "PROFESSION OF SOEUR THÉRÈSE"

SCRIPTURE

For I am the LORD, your God, who grasp your right hand; It is I who say to you, "Do not fear, I will help you."….The afflicted and the needy seek water in vain, their tongues are parched with thirst. I, the LORD, will answer them; I, the God of Israel, will not forsake them.

ISAIAH 41:13,17

As a mother comforts her son, so will I comfort you; in Jerusalem you shall find your comfort.

ISAIAH 66:13

PRAYER

God of love, you provide me all the comfort I need. You lift me up from the darkness and shine the light of your love and mercy upon me. When I fear what is difficult and even consider it to be impossible, it is your love that moves me to action, to share with others the love and comfort you have provided to me. May your love transform my timid self to love beyond fear and darkness, making your love present to those in need of the comfort you have given to me. Amen.

LENTEN ACTION

Is there a person in your life in need of comfort? Is there a person who comes to mind whose life would benefit from knowing the comfort of God, a comfort that can be shared through you? Who do you know personally—or through someone—who is frightened, lost, angry, or grieving? What would a kind word, telephone call, email, or card mean to that person during a period of darkness? Might it shine the light of God's love in that person's life? This small action could make all the difference. Pray that God comfort and guide you as you move to share his comfort and love with just one person!

DAY 6

The Power of Prayer

How wonderful is the power of prayer! It is like unto a queen, who, having free access to the king, obtains whatsoever she asks....

With me, prayer is an uplifting of the heart; a glance toward heaven; a cry of gratitude and love, uttered equally in sorrow and in joy. In a word, it is something noble, supernatural, which expands my soul and unites it to God....Sometimes when I am in such a state of spiritual dryness that not a single good thought occurs to me, I say very slowly the "Our Father" or the "Hail Mary," and these prayers suffice to take me out of myself and wonderfully refresh me.

THE STORY OF A SOUL, X, "THE NEW COMMANDMENT"

Scripture

When you pray, do not be like the hypocrites, who love to stand and pray in the synagogues and on street corners so that others may see them. Amen, I say to you, they have received their reward. But when you pray, go to your inner room, close the door, and pray to your Father in secret. And your Father who sees in secret will repay you. In praying, do not babble like the pagans, who think that they will be heard because of their many words. Do not be like them. Your Father knows what you need before you ask him.

MATTHEW 6:5–8

Prayer

Lord Jesus, my heart is filled with love for you. Though the words to express this love may not come easily, know that despite an inability to voice my love and gratitude, my love and gratitude are there all the same. Even if I do find the proper words, I know these words are still insufficient to express the love we share. May we always love beyond words, for though words are beautiful and poetic at times, they can never compare to the reality of your love or even the love I have for you. I am but a small child and you are my loving Father. Love me, Lord Jesus, and provide for me all that I need. Amen.

Lenten Action

How long has it been since you wrote a prayer? Take time to compose a prayer for the Lord and commit it to paper. Keep this prayer with you so that, even after Lent and Easter have passed, you have with you the words of love you put on paper to express your love and gratitude for the Lord. Include a special intention with your prayer if it suits you. This specific request to the Lord can be something with which you struggle every day. Deliver this struggle or weakness to the Lord for his consideration so he might bless it and grace you with the strength and guidance to approach this struggle with a renewed perspective fashioned by love.

DAY 7

The Prayer of a Child

God in his infinite goodness has given me a clear insight into the deep mysteries of Charity. If I could but express what I know, you would hear a heavenly music; but alas! I can only stammer like a child, and if God's own words were not my support, I should be tempted to beg leave to hold my peace. When the Divine Master tells me to give to whosoever asks of me, and to let what is mine be taken without asking it again, it seems to me that He speaks not only of the goods of earth, but also of the goods of Heaven. Besides, neither one nor the other are really mine; I renounced the former by the vow of poverty, and the latter gifts are simply lent. If God withdraw them, I have no right to complain.

I do as children who have not learnt to read—I simply tell Our Lord all that I want, and He always understands.

The Story of a Soul, X, "The New Commandment"

SCRIPTURE

He was praying in a certain place, and when he had finished, one of his disciples said to him, "Lord, teach us to pray just as John taught his disciples." He said to them, "When you pray, say: Father, hallowed be your name, your kingdom come. Give us each day our daily bread and forgive us our sins for we ourselves forgive everyone in debt to us, and do not subject us to the final test."

LUKE 11:1–4

PRAYER

Good and grace-filled Father, you welcome us by any means when we come to you. Sinners and saints, you love us the same. Rich and poor, we are loved. You delight in the many ways we pray to you—through chant, song, public and private devotion, prayers rich with bountiful verse and flowing prose, and prayers expressed with the simple words of a child. Lord, know that my prayer is my own, whether it was written by someone else or if it comes from my own design. My prayer is my own. My love makes it so. Though words sometimes fail me, you know my heart and you love me all the more for my faults. Amen.

LENTEN ACTION

God gave us the perfect prayer through his Son, our Lord Jesus. Sometimes we say the Our Father in a rushed manner, denying it the attention and reverence it deserves. Take a few minutes to say this prayer deliberately, line by line. Say the Our Father again, this time reflecting on each phrase. Next, journal your thoughts as you read each phrase. Say the prayer one more time, slowly. Pretend you are a child who knows no other way but this prayer to speak to the heavenly Father.

DAY 8

WEDNESDAY OF THE FIRST WEEK OF LENT

Giving the Lord Our Attention in Every Way

*Y*es, they will run—we shall all run together, for souls that are on fire can never be at rest. They may indeed [...] sit at the feet of Jesus, listening to His sweet and burning words, but, though they seem to give Him nothing, they give much more than Martha, who busied herself about many things. It is not Martha's work that Our Lord blames, but her over-solicitude; His Blessed Mother humbly occupied herself in the same kind of work when she prepared the meals for the Holy Family.

THE STORY OF A SOUL, XI, "A CANTICLE OF LOVE"

SCRIPTURE

As they continued their journey he entered a village where a woman whose name was Martha welcomed him. She had a sister named Mary (who) sat beside the Lord at his feet listening to him speak. Martha, burdened with much serving, came to him and said, "Lord, do you not care that my sister has left me by myself to do the serving? Tell her to help me." The Lord said to her in reply, "Martha, Martha, you are anxious and worried about many things. There is need of only one thing. Mary has chosen the better part and it will not be taken from her."

LUKE 10:38–42

PRAYER

Loving Jesus, help me to keep my eyes on you through all my life experiences, be it a storm upon the ocean or my daily tasks of cleaning, caring for my spouse and children, for an elderly parent, or for a dear friend. Help me to dwell not so much on the tedium of the task at hand but on your loving kindness and how my activity can unite me to your love and bring me closer to you. Help me to find your love in all things and to remember that as long as I keep my attention on you, who has graced every facet of human life, I am never without you. Amen.

LENTEN ACTION

During your daily tasks, especially as you complete the routine activities that often fill your day, keep your focus on the Lord and remember how he has graced everything we do through his Incarnation. Make a prayer of your work and your leisure, finding God in everything you do. Keep in conversation with the Lord as you tend to the task at hand and focus your attention on the Lord throughout your day, in everything you do and say, and in *everyone* you encounter along the way.

DAY 9

Reconciling to Our Lord

I have only to open the Holy Gospels and at once I breathe the perfume of Jesus, and then I know which way to run; and it is not to the first place, but to the last, that I hasten. I leave the Pharisee to go up, and full of confidence I repeat the humble prayer of the Publican. Above all I follow Magdalen, for the amazing, rather I should say, the loving audacity that delights the Heart of Jesus has cast its spell upon mine. It is not because I have been preserved from mortal sin that I lift up my heart to God in trust and love. I feel that even had I on my conscience every crime one could commit, I should lose nothing of my confidence: my heart broken with sorrow, I would throw myself into the Arms of my Saviour. I know that He loves the Prodigal Son, I have heard His words to St. Mary Magdalen, to the woman taken in adultery, and to the woman of Samaria. No one could frighten me, for I know what to believe concerning His Mercy and His Love. And I know that all that multitude of sins would disappear in an instant.

THE STORY OF A SOUL, XI, "A CANTICLE OF LOVE"

SCRIPTURE

A clean heart create for me, God;
renew within me a steadfast spirit.
Do not drive me from before your face,
nor take from me your holy spirit.
Restore to me the gladness of your salvation;
uphold me with a willing spirit.
I will teach the wicked your ways,
that sinners may return to you..

PSALM 51:12–15

PRAYER

Oh, loving and tender God, there is nothing I can hide from you. Every part of me is laid bare. You see me for everything I am and everything I can be with your grace. When I sin, when I fall, you raise me up and you bring me closer to you than I was before I had fallen. Grant me, loving and tender God, the grace to bring to you everything I am, my self with all my faults, that you might create in me a clean heart and bring me ever closer to you that I might sing your praises and inspire others to come to you in a like manner. Amen.

LENTEN ACTION

Spend five to ten minutes in reflection on the following questions: How do I regard my own sinfulness? Do I view it with disdain? With embarrassment? Do I share my sinful thoughts and actions in prayer with God? Do I share this with God in a spirit of asking for forgiveness? Do I share this with God as a means to bring myself closer to God by relying on him to cleanse me from my sin, to draw me closer, and to restore in me a clean and willing spirit? With this view of sin and my relationship with God, how might I be moved to share this insight with my fellow brothers and sisters?

DAY 10

FRIDAY OF THE FIRST WEEK OF LENT

Full Confidence in His Mercy

J had grieved her, and had gone to ask her pardon: "If you but knew what I feel!" she exclaimed. "Never have I more clearly understood the love with which Jesus receives us when we seek His forgiveness. If I, His poor little creature, feel so tenderly toward you when you come back to me, what must pass through Our Lord's Divine Heart when we return to Him? Far more quickly than I have just done will He blot out our sins from His memory….Nay, He will even love us more tenderly than before we fell."

THE STORY OF A SOUL, "COUNSELS AND REMINISCENCES OF SOEUR THÉRÈSE"

SCRIPTURE

You were dead in your transgressions and sins in which you once lived following the age of this world, following the ruler of the power of the air, the spirit that is now at work in the disobedient. All of us once lived among them in the desires of our flesh, following the wishes of the flesh and the impulses, and we were by nature children of wrath, like the rest. But God, who is rich in mercy, because of the great love he had for us, even when we were dead in our transgressions, brought us to life with Christ (by grace you have been saved), raised us up with him, and seated us with him in the heavens in Christ Jesus, that in the ages to come he might show the immeasurable riches of his grace in his kindness to us in Christ Jesus. For by grace you have been saved through faith....

EPHESIANS 2:1–8

PRAYER

Merciful God, I thank you for loving me beyond my failings, for drawing me near to you after I willingly turned from your loving face. You have created in me a loving heart, a heart that loves in the way your Son loves the world, in the way you taught us to love. I ask that you grace me with the passion to love others as you love me. I pray that you grace me to act with the passion by which your Son performed his works of love and compassion. I pray that I see the world the way you see it, Lord, and that I perform good works in response to the love and compassion that springs forth from the source of all love, namely, you. Amen.

LENTEN ACTION

As you go about your day today, ask that God grace you with the ability to view his creation through his loving and compassionate eyes. When you see the world through his eyes, you will know how to respond. You will respond in the manner our Lord and Savior responded when he saw the world during his time upon this earth as a man. Reach out to your brothers and sisters in this manner, respond to every need you encounter in a spirit of compassion and love. Perform your actions with full confidence in God's mercy. Know that you are able to love in this manner because God has loved you beyond your faults, and you are called to love others in a manner that sees beyond any faults they have and in any ways they may have hurt you in the past.

DAY 11

God Loves Others Through Us

*A*fter receiving this grace my desire for the salvation of souls increased day by day. I seemed to hear Our Lord whispering to me, as He did to the Samaritan woman: "Give me to drink!" (John 4:7) It was indeed an exchange of love: upon souls I poured forth the Precious Blood of Jesus, and to Jesus I offered these souls refreshed with the Dew of Calvary. In this way I thought to quench His Thirst; but the more I gave Him to drink, so much the more did the thirst of my own poor soul increase, and I accepted it as the most delightful recompense.

THE STORY OF A SOUL, V, "VOCATION OF THÉRÈSE"

SCRIPTURE

But because he wished to justify himself, he said to Jesus, "And who is my neighbor?" Jesus replied, "A man fell victim to robbers as he went down from Jerusalem to Jericho. They stripped and beat him and went off leaving him half-dead. A priest happened to be going down that road, but when he saw him, he passed by on the opposite side. Likewise a Levite came to the place, and when he saw him, he passed by on the opposite side. But a Samaritan traveler who came upon him was moved with compassion at the sight. He approached the victim, poured oil and wine over his wounds and bandaged them. Then he lifted him up on his own animal, took him to an inn and cared for him. The next day he took out two silver coins and gave them to the innkeeper with the instruction, 'Take care of him. If you spend more than what I have given you, I shall repay you on my way back.' Which of these three, in your opinion, was neighbor to the robbers' victim?" He answered, "The one who treated him with mercy." Jesus said to him, "Go and do likewise."

LUKE 10:29–37

PRAYER

Lord, give me the insight not only to see the person in need but to see with that person what he or she needs to live a life of dignity, security, peace, and joy. In response to the teachings of your Son, may I serve those in need and call others to do the same. As the Good Samaritan gave his love to the one he met by chance along the road, may I reach out to my brothers and sisters in a like manner, regardless of their race, creed, or ethnic background. Amen.

LENTEN ACTION

To include the excluded: That, some say, is one of the hardest things for a person to do. We are so accustomed to our own class, our own kind, that we rarely challenge ourselves to extend our love beyond where we are and what we know. Make a point to reach out to someone who is outside your circle of friends, beyond your parish boundaries, beyond your comfort zone. This means you taking the first step and letting someone know he is loved and thought of during this Lenten season. With God's grace acting through you, you can make someone outside your circle, perhaps someone who feels unloved, know that he is loved.

DAY 12

Keep Your Eyes Set on the Lord

*L*ast night I was seized with a terrible feeling of anguish," she confessed to Mother Agnes of Jesus on one occasion; "I was lost in darkness, and from out of it came an accursed voice: 'Are you certain God loves you? Has He Himself told you so? The opinion of creatures will not justify you in His sight.' These thoughts had long tortured me, when your little note, like a message from Heaven, was brought to me. You recalled to me, dear Mother, the special graces Jesus had lavished upon me, and, as though you had had a revelation concerning my trial, you assured me I was deeply loved by God and was on the eve of receiving from His Hands my eternal crown. Immediately peace and joy were restored to my heart. Yet the thought came to me, 'It is my little Mother's affection that makes her write these words.' I felt inspired to take up the Gospels, and, opening the book at random, I lighted on [this]passage: 'He whom God hath sent speaketh the Words of God, for God doth not give the Spirit by measure.' Then I fell asleep fully consoled."

THE STORY OF A SOUL, "EPILOGUE"

SCRIPTURE

Then he made the disciples get into the boat and precede him to the other side, while he dismissed the crowds. After doing so, he went up on the mountain by himself to pray. When it was evening he was there alone. Meanwhile the boat, already a few miles offshore, was being tossed about by the waves, for the wind was against it. During the fourth watch of the night, he came toward them, walking on the sea. When the disciples saw him walking on the sea they were terrified. "It is a ghost," they said, and they cried out in fear. At once (Jesus) spoke to them, "Take courage, it is I; do not be afraid."

Peter said to him in reply, "Lord, if it is you, command me to come to you on the water." He said, "Come." Peter got out of the boat and began to walk on the water toward Jesus. But when he saw how (strong) the wind was he became frightened; and, beginning to sink, he cried out, "Lord, save me!" Immediately Jesus stretched out his hand and caught him, and said to him, "O you of little faith, why did you doubt?" After they got into the boat, the wind died down. Those who were in the boat did him homage, saying, "Truly, you are the Son of God."

MATTHEW 14:22–33

PRAYER

Good and loving Lord Jesus, grant me the strength and resolve to keep my eyes on your loving gaze at all times. When I am focused on you, dear Lord, I do not dwell on fear or on what is impossible. When I am centered on you, there is no place for fear and all things are possible. I am your instrument, Lord; use me as you will. I can do great things through you, as your instrument, for the sake of your creation. Move me and guide me to do your will, oh Lord, and when I stray I know you will call out my name and my eyes will find you there, always ready to take my hand and lead me where I need to be, according to your will. Amen.

LENTEN ACTION

Reread the Scripture passage above and imagine yourself as Peter. Reflect on this scene and recall moments from your own life when you took your eyes off the Lord and went out on your own. Were you frightened? Did you fall? Did you feel alone? Did difficult things seem impossible? Did your actions seem self-serving, without purpose? Now recall those times when you kept yourself focused on the Lord, when you were centered and at peace with him. Did you feel safe and secure? Did you feel his guidance? Are you aware that despite how many times you falter or turn your gaze from the Lord that he is there waiting for you with his hand reaching for yours? Reflect in silence on the fact that you can do great things when the Lord guides you and that your life becomes easier and less taxing when the Lord lifts the yoke from your shoulders and allows you to serve his creation according to his will.

DAY 13

MONDAY OF THE SECOND WEEK OF LENT

Make Yourself a Suitable Dwelling Place for the Lord

*L*et me suppose that I had been born in a land of thick fogs and had never seen the beauties of nature or a single ray of sunshine, although I had heard of these wonders from my early youth and knew that the country wherein I dwelt was not my real home—there was another land unto which I should always look forward....

From the time of my childhood I felt that one day I should be set free from this land of darkness. I believed it, not only because I had been told so by others, but my heart's most secret and deepest longings assured me that there was in store for me another and more beautiful country—an abiding dwelling place. I was like Christopher Columbus, whose genius anticipated the discovery of the New World.

THE STORY OF A SOUL, IX, "THE NIGHT OF THE SOUL"

SCRIPTURE

According to the grace of God given to me, like a wise master builder I laid a foundation, and another is building upon it. But each one must be careful how he builds upon it, for no one can lay a foundation other than the one that is there, namely, Jesus Christ. If anyone builds on this foundation with gold, silver, precious stones, wood, hay, or straw, the work of each will come to light, for the Day will disclose it. It will be revealed with fire, and the fire (itself) will test the quality of each one's work. If the work stands that someone built upon the foundation, that person will receive a wage. But if someone's work is burned up, that one will suffer loss; the person will be saved, but only as through fire. Do you not know that you are the temple of God, and that the Spirit of God dwells in you? If anyone destroys God's temple, God will destroy that person; for the temple of God, which you are, is holy.

1 CORINTHIANS 3:10–17

PRAYER

Generous God, you have crafted me in your own image. My humanity has been made sacred by the sacrifice of your Son. I am indeed a dwelling place for you, Lord, a temple where your goodness resides. You are the builder, Lord, and your foundation is Jesus Christ and his love, the strongest foundation there is, one that is lasting and eternal. May you always dwell inside of me, Lord. May you always call me your temple and your home. Amen.

LENTEN ACTION

For your daily action, reflect on your body as "God's temple" as a dwelling place for the Lord. It is our responsibility to care for our bodies—for the life we've been given—to the best of our ability. We are called to be good stewards of our bodies. Make a list of those ways that you care for your body and another list of ways you can serve your body in a manner more befitting its value as a gift from God.

DAY 14

TUESDAY OF THE SECOND WEEK OF LENT

Let Us Hear the Word of God With the Trust of a Child

About this time Our Lord gave me the consolation of an intimate knowledge of the souls of children. I gained it in this way. During the illness of a poor woman, I interested myself in her two little girls, the elder of whom was not yet six. It was a real pleasure to see how simply they believed all that I told them. Baptism does indeed plant deeply in our souls the theological virtues, since from early childhood the hope of heavenly reward is strong enough to make us practice self-denial. When I wanted my two little girls to be especially kind to one another, instead of promising them toys and sweets, I talked to them about the eternal recompense the Holy Child Jesus would give to good children. The elder one, who was coming to the use of reason, used to look quite pleased and asked me charming questions about the little Jesus and His beautiful Heaven. She promised me faithfully always to give in to her little sister, adding that all through her life she would never forget what I had taught her.

I used to compare these innocent souls to soft wax, ready to receive any impression—evil, alas, as well as good, and I understood the words of Our Lord: "It were better to be thrown into the sea than to scandalize one of these little ones" (see Matthew 18:6).

THE STORY OF A SOUL, V, "VOCATION OF THÉRÈSE"

SCRIPTURE

> *Blessed are those who trust in the LORD;*
> *the LORD will be their trust.*
> *They are like a tree planted beside the waters*
> *that stretches out its roots to the stream:*
> *It does not fear heat when it comes,*
> *its leaves stay green;*
> *In the year of drought it shows no distress,*
> *but still produces fruit.*

JEREMIAH 17:7–8

> *Trust in the LORD with all your heart, on your own intelligence*
> *do not rely; In all your ways be mindful of him, and he will make*
> *straight your paths.*

PROVERBS 3:5–6

PRAYER

Lord, help me to find you in the simplest of things: in the face and voice of a child, in a sunrise and a sunset, in a cold drink of water, and in the silence of the night. Make your presence known to me as I go about the simplest of things and, even when I feel spiritually parched and without a friend, grace me with the comfort and knowledge that you are with me then. May I trust in you always and may nothing stand in the way of my giving myself completely to you. Amen.

LENTEN ACTION

Read Matthew 14:22–33 with the eyes of a child and marvel at the miracle performed by our Lord Jesus Christ as he walks upon the water toward the boat that holds the apostles. Reflect on the trust Jesus seeks from his apostles and see how Peter expresses great trust in Jesus, a childlike trust, but when he turns his simple, direct gaze from the Lord and focuses on the storm, that is, the complications of life, he sinks into the raging waters. Jesus is quick to save Peter but he wonders why his apostle feels doubt and a lack of trust when in the presence of the Lord.

DAY 15

To Give Without Asking in Return

There are, of course, no enemies in the Carmel; but, after all, we have our natural likes and dislikes. We may feel drawn toward one Sister and may be tempted to go a long way round to avoid meeting another. Well, Our Lord tells me that this is the Sister to love and pray for, even though her behaviour may make me imagine she does not care for me. "If you love them that love you, what thanks are to you? For sinners also love those that love them" (Luke 6:32). And it is not enough to love, we must prove our love; naturally one likes to please a friend, but that is not charity, for sinners do the same....

To give to everyone who asks is not so pleasant as to give of one's own accord. If we are asked pleasantly, it is easy to give; but if we are asked discourteously, then, unless we are perfect in charity, there is an inward rebellion, and we find no end of excuses for refusing....I say this is hard, but I should rather say that it seems hard, for "the yoke of the Lord is sweet and His burden light" (Matthew 11:30). And when we submit to that yoke, we at once feel its sweetness.

THE STORY OF A SOUL, IX, "THE NIGHT OF THE SOUL"

SCRIPTURE

What good is it, my brothers, if someone says he has faith but does not have works? Can that faith save him? If a brother or sister has nothing to wear and has no food for the day, and one of you says to them, "Go in peace, keep warm, and eat well," but you do not give them the necessities of the body, what good is it? So also faith of itself, if it does not have works, is dead. Indeed someone might say, "You have faith and I have works." Demonstrate your faith to me without works, and I will demonstrate my faith to you from my works. Was not Abraham our father justified by works when he offered his son Isaac upon the altar? You see that faith was active along with his works, and faith was completed by the works.

JAMES 2:14–18, 21–22

PRAYER

Lord God, you who gives to us unceasingly, move my heart to approach those in need in a like manner. May I never expect a return on anything I give. May my giving only bring me closer to you, the source of all love. Move me to provide for my brother and sister in need so that my faith in you is strengthened by the loving work done by you through me, your humble instrument. I ask that you open my heart and my eyes in seeing those in need, and I ask that you move me to act in accord with your will. Amen.

LENTEN ACTION

Seek out need in your parish or elsewhere in or outside of your neighborhood. Resources are available to direct you to that need—through your parish and various charities in your community that seek volunteers. A little research and a few well-pointed questions are all you need to find a person who needs your help. Give yourself completely to your work and see how it strengthens your faith and your relationship with the Lord. Ask God to help you see with eyes of love, and God will direct you where your help is needed most.

DAY 16

Knock and the Door Will Be Opened to You

I have not told you all my thoughts on this passage of the Sacred Canticles: "Draw me—we will run!"

Our Lord has said: "No man can come to Me except the Father Who hath sent Me, draw him" (John 6:44), and later He tells us that whosoever seeks shall find, whosoever asks shall receive, that unto him that knocks it shall be opened, and He adds that whatever we ask the Father in His Name shall be given us (see John 16:23).

It was no doubt for this reason that, long before the birth of Our Lord, the Holy Spirit dictated these prophetic words: "Draw me—we will run!" By asking to be drawn, we desire an intimate union with the object of our love.

THE STORY OF A SOUL, XI, "A CANTICLE OF LOVE"

SCRIPTURE

"I have told you this in figures of speech. The hour is coming when I will no longer speak to you in figures but I will tell you clearly about the Father. On that day you will ask in my name,

and I do not tell you that I will ask the Father for you. For the Father himself loves you, because you have loved me and have come to believe that I came from God. I came from the Father and have come into the world. Now I am leaving the world and going back to the Father....Do you believe now? Behold, the hour is coming and has arrived when each of you will be scattered to his own home and you will leave me alone. But I am not alone, because the Father is with me. I have told you this so that you might have peace in me. In the world you will have trouble, but take courage, I have conquered the world."

JOHN 16:25–28, 31–33

PRAYER

Loving and caring Lord, you tell us to "ask in [your] name." I ask that you guide me to want what is necessary and fulfilling to desire, all that benefits me as your creation. You know what is best for me and that is all I desire. Guide me, Lord, to pursue only those things in this world that bring me closer to you, closer to love, closer to understanding who I am and what I can provide for others who seek to know you through my thoughts, words, and actions. Use me, Lord, as an extension of your love, and keep me close to your heart at all times. I ask this of you, Lord, in your name. Amen.

LENTEN ACTION

Today, do your best to model the love the Lord has for all people you encounter. Listen to them, offer to assist them in any way you can, and remind them that they are loved by the Lord. View yourself as an instrument of the Lord in all you do or say. Before you are about to assist someone, however, ask Jesus how he would like you to respond. Ask him as simply as this: "Lord Jesus, how do you want me to respond to this person? Give me the guidance, Jesus, to understand this person and what he or she needs. Move me to respond to this person in the manner you would, and channel your love through me, your instrument, to this person in need.

DAY 17

Give Back to God All He Has Given to You

*Y*et all souls cannot be alike. It is necessary that they should differ from one another in order that each Divine Perfection may receive its special honour. To me, He has given His Infinite Mercy, and it is in this ineffable mirror that I contemplate his other attributes. Therein all appear to me radiant with Love. His Justice, even more perhaps than the rest, seems to me to be clothed with Love. What joy to think that Our Lord is just, that is to say, that He takes our weakness into account, that He knows perfectly the frailty of our nature! Of what, then, need I be afraid?

THE STORY OF A SOUL, VIII, "PROFESSION OF SOEUR THÉRÈSE"

SCRIPTURE

Moreover, God is able to make every grace abundant for you,
so that in all things, always having all you need, you may have
an abundance for every good work....You are being enriched in
every way for all generosity, which through us produces thanks-
giving to God, for the administration of this public service is not
only supplying the needs of the holy ones but is also overflowing
in many acts of thanksgiving to God. Through the evidence of
this service, you are glorifying God for your obedient confession
of the gospel of Christ and the generosity of your contribution
to them and to all others, while in prayer on your behalf they
long for you, because of the surpassing grace of God upon you.
Thanks be to God for his indescribable gift!

2 CORINTHIANS 9: 8, 11–15

PRAYER

Father, love through me, care for your creation through me, your
willing instrument. I am at your disposal to do anything you ask of
me. May I see your face as I look into the faces of my brothers and
sisters; may I keep you in my heart as I go about my daily duties,
offering every action and every breath in praise of your holy name.
May I spread the word of your good news and may everyone know
your love by my every action without my saying a word. Amen.

LENTEN ACTION

When I encounter someone new, do I try to see the face of Jesus in
him or her? What aspects do I notice first? Do I dwell on negative
characteristics? Or do I see the best things? Make an effort to view a
person as God would, focusing on all those parts of the person that
make him or her special and lovable. Dismiss any negative thoughts
that might crop up. Pray that God bless you with this vision, that
he might grant you the grace to see with loving eyes. Practice this
exercise on those people who irritate you as well!

DAY 18

SATURDAY OF THE SECOND WEEK OF LENT

Responding Joyfully When Asked

I remember an act of charity with which God inspired me while I was still a novice, and this act, though seemingly small, has been rewarded even in this life by Our Heavenly Father, "Who seeth in secret."

Shortly before Sister St. Peter became quite bedridden, it was necessary every evening, at ten minutes to six, for someone to leave meditation and take her to the refectory. It cost me a good deal to offer my services, for I knew the difficulty, or I should say the impossibility, of pleasing the poor invalid. But I did not want to lose such a good opportunity, for I recalled Our Lord's words: "As long as you did it to one of these my least brethren, you did it to Me" (Matthew 25:40). I therefore humbly offered my aid. It was not without difficulty I induced her to accept it, but after considerable persuasion I succeeded....I had to follow the good Sister, supporting her by her girdle; I did it as gently as possible, but if by some mischance she stumbled, she imagined I had not a firm hold, and that she was going to fall. "You are going too fast," she would say, "I shall fall and hurt myself!" Then when I tried to lead her more quietly: "Come quicker...I cannot feel you...you are letting me go! I was right when I said you were too young to take care of me."

When we reached the refectory...I soon noticed that she found it very difficult to cut her bread, so I did not leave her till I had performed this last service. She was much touched by this attention on my part, for she had not expressed any wish on the subject; it was by this unsought-for kindness that I gained her entire confidence, and chiefly because—as I learnt later—at the end of my humble task I bestowed upon her my sweetest smile.

THE STORY OF A SOUL, X, "THE NEW COMMANDMENT"

SCRIPTURE

[Jesus said,] "Give to everyone who asks of you, and from the one who takes what is yours do not demand it back. Do to others as you would have them do to you. For if you love those who love you, what credit is that to you? Even sinners love those who love them. And if you do good to those who do good to you, what credit is that to you? Even sinners do the same. If you lend money to those from whom you expect repayment, what credit (is) that to you? Even sinners lend to sinners, and get back the same amount. But rather, love your enemies and do good to them, and lend expecting nothing back; then your reward will be great and you will be children of the Most High, for he himself is kind to the ungrateful and the wicked. Be merciful, just as (also) your Father is merciful."

LUKE 6:30–36

PRAYER

Lord of mercy and kindness, love your creation through me. Where there is need, direct me. Where there is someone in need of comfort or a listening ear, direct me there. Let your love be known to everyone I meet and serve. I am your willing instrument; may your will be one with my own so that I know where you want your love expressed through me. I ask only to be led by your loving hand. I am your willing servant; use me as you will. Amen.

LENTEN ACTION

How do you respond when you see a person in need? Do you hesitate to help? Do you judge? Make it a point to throw yourself into a situation that calls for your immediate response. Do not sit and question the situation but allow God to direct you as you respond with his love as an instrument of his kindness and compassion. You will know it is God acting through you as your will acquiesces to his own. The peace this provides is beyond measure.

DAY 19

Follow Him and Fish for People

*H*ow happy does Our Lord make me, and how sweet and easy is his service on this earth! He has always given me what I desired, or rather He has made me desire what He wishes to give.

THE STORY OF A SOUL, X, "THE NEW COMMANDMENT"

*F*rom afar it seems so easy to do good to souls, to teach them to love God more, and to model them according to one's own ideas. But, when we draw nearer, we quickly feel that without God's help this is quite as impossible as to bring back the sun when once it has set. We must forget ourselves, and put aside our tastes and ideas, and guide souls not by our own way, but along the path which Our Lord points out.

THE STORY OF A SOUL, X, "THE NEW COMMANDMENT"

SCRIPTURE

As he was walking by the Sea of Galilee, he saw two brothers, Simon who is called Peter, and his brother Andrew, casting a net into the sea; they were fishermen. He said to them, "Come after me, and I will make you fishers of men." At once they left their nets and followed him. He walked along from there and saw two other brothers, James, the son of Zebedee, and his brother John. They were in a boat, with their father Zebedee, mending their nets. He called them, and immediately they left their boat and their father and followed him.

MATTHEW 4:18–22

PRAYER

Dear Lord, you guide me in all ways and, by your grace, I come to know you in all things good and holy. Today I ask for the grace to recommit myself to you, to give up everything I have—all temporal treasures and all attachments—that keeps me from giving myself completely to you. I ask that you make me a "fisher of men" a "fisher of all people," and that my lack of attachments to all things worldly will bring others ever closer to you by their understanding of me and the witness I display thanks to your grace. Amen.

LENTEN ACTION

Consider those items in your life that make it difficult for you to give your full attention God. Perhaps too much time devoted to electronic devices (cell phones, television, radio, and the internet, for example) has left you somewhat numb and unresponsive to the voice of God or the calls for attention from those in greatest need. Make it a point to reduce the amount of time you give to electronic devices and turn your attention to everything that is going on around you, the people you encounter throughout your day, what God is encouraging you to do in response to their need to be heard and engaged.

DAY 20

He Gives to Us in Abundance

*I*n truth I am no Saint, as this frame of mind well shows. I ought not to rejoice in my dryness of soul, but rather attribute it to my want of fervour and fidelity. That I fall asleep so often during meditation, and thanksgiving after Communion, should distress me. Well, I am not distressed. I reflect that little children are equally dear to their parents whether they are asleep or awake....

[During a recent retreat] I unconsciously received many interior lights on the best means of pleasing God, and practicing virtue. I have often observed that Our Lord will not give me any store of provisions, but nourishes me each moment with food that is ever new; I find it within me without knowing how it has come there. I simply believe that it is Jesus Himself hidden in my poor heart who is secretly at work, inspiring me with what He wishes me to do as each occasion arises.

THE STORY OF A SOUL, VIII, "PROFESSION OF SOEUR THÉRÈSE"

SCRIPTURE

Together were Simon Peter, Thomas called Didymus, Nathanael from Cana in Galilee, Zebedee's sons, and two other of his disciples. Simon Peter said to them, "I am going fishing." They said to him, "We also will come with you." So they went out and got into the boat, but that night they caught nothing. When it was already dawn, Jesus was standing on the shore; but the disciples did not realize that it was Jesus. Jesus said to them, "Children, have you caught anything to eat?" They answered him, "No." So he said to them, "Cast the net over the right side of the boat and you will find something." So they cast it, and were not able to pull it in because of the number of fish. So the disciple whom Jesus loved said to Peter, "It is the Lord."

JOHN 21:2–7

PRAYER

Loving and generous Lord, who gives me everything I desire and more, I thank you for all that you provide me—throughout my days, weeks, and months—as I live my life according to your will. I am grateful that you are always there for me when I need you most, and that—when I call upon you for strength to persevere—you feed me and nourish me from a wellspring of unending love and generosity. I know that you will never leave my side, loving God, and because of this overwhelming store of provisions, I thank you through everything I think, say, and do in your loving name. Amen.

LENTEN ACTION

How often do you bear witness to the love and generosity the Lord grants you? Today, express your gratitude to God for his unending grace. Speak with people close to you about how the Lord guides you throughout your day, how you offer up your struggles to the Lord in moments of difficulty and indecision, and how God provides for you as you seek to fulfill his will. Listen closely to these people as they share with you their own struggles and help them recognize how the Lord is providing for them in their own times of need.

DAY 21

TUESDAY OF THE THIRD WEEK OF LENT

His Will Be Done

O my God! from how much disquiet do we free ourselves by the vow of obedience! Happy is the simple religious. Her one guide being the will of her superiors, she is ever sure of following the right path, and has no fear of being mistaken, even when it seems that her superiors are making a mistake. But if she ceases to consult the unerring compass, then at once her soul goes astray in barren wastes, where the waters of grace quickly fail. Dear Mother, you are the compass Jesus has given me to direct me safely to the Eternal Shore. I find it most sweet to fix my eyes upon you, and then do the Will of my Lord. By allowing me to suffer these temptations against Faith, He has greatly increased the spirit of Faith, which makes me see Him living in your soul, and through you communicating His holy commands.

THE STORY OF A SOUL, IX, "THE NIGHT OF THE SOUL"

SCRIPTURE

*He destined us for adoption to himself through Jesus Christ,
in accord with the favor of his will, for the praise of the glory
of his grace that he granted us in the beloved. In him we have
redemption by his blood, the forgiveness of transgressions, in
accord with the riches of his grace that he lavished upon us. In
all wisdom and insight, he has made known to us the mystery
of his will in accord with his favor that he set forth in him as a
plan for the fullness of times, to sum up all things in Christ, in
heaven and on earth. In him we were also chosen, destined in
accord with the purpose of the one who accomplishes all things
according to the intention of his will, so that we might exist for
the praise of his glory, we who first hoped in Christ.*

EPHESIANS 1:5–12

PRAYER

Loving Father, it is your will that I seek to know and your will that
I seek to do throughout my day. Guide me in that direction, Lord.
Help me to know your will through the sacraments, through the
Mass, through holy Scripture, and anything else you can provide
me. And when I know your will, Lord, grace me with the strength
and perseverance to do your will so that your love might be known
through me, your willing servant. Amen.

LENTEN ACTION

Take a few minutes today to pray the Our Father several times. Take
a pen and paper and write the prayer down. Circle three passages
that speak to you in particular. Dwell on these passages in depth,
pray on them, use them to see the world as you go about the rest of
the day's activities. How do these words affect your view of others, of
God, of what God is asking you to do? If it is evening while you are at
prayer, make it a point to adopt this "Lenten Action" for tomorrow.

DAY 22

May I Give Myself in Glory to God

*A*nd yet never have I felt so deeply how sweet and merciful is the Lord. He did not send me this heavy cross when it might have discouraged me, but at a time when I was able to bear it. Now it simply takes from me all natural satisfaction I might feel in my longing for Heaven.

Dear Mother, it seems to me that at present there is nothing to impede my upward flight, for I have no longer any desire save to love Him till I die. I am free; I fear nothing now, not even what I dreaded more than anything else, a long illness which would make me a burden to the Community. Should it please the Good God, I am quite content to have my bodily and mental sufferings prolonged for years. I do not fear a long life; I do not shrink from the struggle. The Lord is the rock upon which I stand—"Who teacheth my hands to fight, and my fingers to war. He is my Protector and I have hoped in Him." (Psalm 144:1–2) I have never asked God to let me die young, It is true I have always thought I should do so, but it is a favour I have not tried to obtain.

THE STORY OF A SOUL, IX, "THE NIGHT OF THE SOUL"

SCRIPTURE

We ask you, brothers, to respect those who are laboring among you and who are over you in the Lord and who admonish you, and to show esteem for them with special love on account of their work. Be at peace among yourselves. We urge you, brothers, admonish the idle, cheer the fainthearted, support the weak, be patient with all. See that no one returns evil for evil; rather, always seek what is good (both) for each other and for all. Rejoice always. Pray without ceasing. In all circumstances give thanks, for this is the will of God for you in Christ Jesus. Do not quench the Spirit. Do not despise prophetic utterances. Test everything; retain what is good. Refrain from every kind of evil.

1 THESSALONIANS 5:12–22

PRAYER

Good and loving God, there are times when I feel I have nothing to offer you, as if you need anything from me. But when I do feel as if I am walking through a spiritual desert, I feel very alone and I am disheartened when I think that this "desert experience" is a result of something lacking in me. Generous Father, you know well that these are the times when I need you most and I should never doubt your presence when I feel alone. Help me to realize that during my feelings of loneliness you are even closer to me, even if I have difficulty seeing that. Amen.

LENTEN ACTION

Do you know someone who has been "down in the dumps" lately? Perhaps he or she is feeling lonely, depressed, or sad. Perhaps responsibilities have begun to weigh down the person, and perhaps he or she feels that God is far away. Make some time in your day to reach out to this person: give him or her a call, offer to help or just let her or him know he or she is appreciated and loved. Serve as God's instrument to a person who feels God is far away.

DAY 23

God Exalts the Humble Heart

O my only Friend, why dost Thou not reserve these infinite longings to lofty souls, to the eagles that soar in the heights? Alas! I am but a poor little unfledged bird. I am not an eagle, I have but the eagle's eyes and heart! Yet, notwithstanding my exceeding littleness, I dare to gaze upon the Divine Sun of Love, and I burn to dart upwards unto Him! I would fly, I would imitate the eagles; but all that I can do is to lift up my little wings—it is beyond my feeble power to soar. What is to become of me? Must I die of sorrow because of my helplessness? Oh, no! I will not even grieve. With daring self-abandonment there will I remain until death, my gaze fixed upon that Divine Sun.

THE STORY OF A SOUL, XI, "A CANTICLE OF LOVE"

SCRIPTURE

Tend the flock of God in your midst, (overseeing) not by con-
straint but willingly, as God would have it, not for shameful
profit but eagerly. Do not lord it over those assigned to you,
but be examples to the flock. And when the chief Shepherd is
revealed, you will receive the unfading crown of glory. Likewise,
you younger members, be subject to the presbyters. And all of
you, clothe yourselves with humility in your dealings with one
another, for: "God opposes the proud but bestows favor on the
humble." So humble yourselves under the mighty hand of God,
that he may exalt you in due time. Cast all your worries upon
him because he cares for you.

1 PETER 5:2–7

PRAYER

Lord, you are the only one who can lift me to the heights I desire.
Whether I am an eagle or a baby bird, I cannot fly to those heights
alone. In either case, be a person great or small, your grace is the
only source of strength that can bring a person, someone you loved
into existence, to your side, both on earth and in Heaven. Loving
Lord, lift me up where I belong, beside the greatest Love I will ever
know, beyond anything anyone can conceive. Amen.

LENTEN ACTION

Today or soon, engage yourself in a "dirty job," a task you regularly
perform with some disdain or an errand you've been known to put
off until tomorrow because you honestly do not want to do it, even
though it must be done. Immerse yourself in this job, that is, do it
thoroughly and with great gusto. Keep in mind your love for God
during this time. Connect the beauty and goodness of your Creator
with a task as humble as one can imagine. Perform this task knowing
full well that it is the Lord who loves us, not despite our lowliness
but because of it. Thérèse knows so well that God desires to embrace
and lift up the "little fledgling."

DAY 24

FRIDAY OF THE THIRD WEEK OF LENT

Make Room in Your Soul for Jesus Alone

I have told you of the first piece of work which you accomplished together with Our Lord by means of the little brush, but that was only the prelude to the masterpiece which was afterwards to be painted. From the moment I entered the sanctuary of souls, I saw at a glance that the task was beyond my strength. Throwing myself without delay into Our Lord's Arms, I imitated those tiny children, who, when they are frightened, hide their faces on their father's shoulder, and I said:

"Dear Lord, Thou seest that I am too small to feed these little ones, but if through me Thou wilt give to each what is suitable, then fill my hands, and without leaving the shelter of Thine Arms or even turning away, I will distribute Thy treasures to the souls who come to me asking for food. Should they find it to their taste, I shall know that this is due not to me, but to Thee; and if, on the contrary, they find fault with its bitterness, I shall not be cast down, but try to persuade them that it cometh from Thee, while taking good care to make no change in it."

The knowledge that it was impossible to do anything of myself rendered my task easier. My one interior occupation was to unite myself more and more closely to God, knowing that the rest would be given to me over and above. And indeed my hope has never been deceived; I have always found my hands filled when sustenance was needed for the souls of my Sisters. But had I done otherwise, and relied on my own strength, I should very soon have been forced to abandon my task.

THE STORY OF A SOUL, X, "THE NEW COMMANDMENT"

SCRIPTURE

Now the snake was the most cunning of all the wild animals that the LORD God had made. He asked the woman, "Did God really say, 'You shall not eat from any of the trees in the garden'?" The woman answered the snake: "We may eat of the fruit of the trees in the garden; it is only about the fruit of the tree in the middle of the garden that God said, 'You shall not eat it or even touch it, or else you will die.'" But the snake said to the woman: "You certainly will not die! God knows well that when you eat of it your eyes will be opened and you will be like gods, who know good and evil."

GENESIS 3:1–5

PRAYER

Great and loving God, allow your love to shine into my heart and keep my eyes trained on you and you alone. Do not allow any doubt or evil to enter my mind and help me to keep my mind on positive thoughts about you, others, and the whole of your creation. Move my heart in this direction so I might be with you when my time on this earth has finished according to your will. I ask this in the name of your loving Son, my Lord Jesus Christ. Amen.

LENTEN ACTION

Consider attending a Stations of the Cross service at your local parish today or on an upcoming Friday during this season of Lent. Go by yourself or with a group. If you have children, bring them with you. The love of God can shine through in a powerful manner during the Stations of the Cross. Invite the Lord to strengthen your resolve to continually make room in your heart for his presence, guidance, and loving will

DAY 25

SATURDAY OF THE THIRD WEEK OF LENT

Trials and Testing

*A*nother time I was working in the laundry, and the Sister opposite, while washing handkerchiefs, repeatedly splashed me with dirty water. My first impulse was to draw back and wipe my face, to show the offender I should be glad if she would behave more quietly; but the next minute I thought how foolish it was to refuse the treasures God offered me so generously, and I refrained from betraying my annoyance. On the contrary, I made such efforts to welcome the shower of dirty water, that at the end of half an hour I had taken quite a fancy to this novel kind of aspersion, and I resolved to come as often as I could to the happy spot where such treasures were freely bestowed.

THE STORY OF A SOUL, XI, "A CANTICLE OF LOVE"

SCRIPTURE

Blessed be the God and Father of our Lord Jesus Christ, the Father of compassion and God of all encouragement, who encourages us in our every affliction, so that we may be able to encourage those who are in any affliction with the encouragement with which we ourselves are encouraged by God. For as Christ's sufferings overflow to us, so through Christ does our encouragement also overflow. If we are afflicted, it is for your encouragement and salvation; if we are encouraged, it is for your encouragement, which enables you to endure the same sufferings that we suffer. Our hope for you is firm, for we know that as you share in the sufferings, you also share in the encouragement.

2 CORINTHIANS 1:3–7

PRAYER

Lord Jesus Christ, you know so well the suffering and torment we experience in our earthly lives. We can become sick or injured in this world. We can suffer chronic pain or face the difficulty of watching a loved one become sick or suffer. It is your consolation that pulls us through to the light of hope, the understanding that our sufferings are not for naught. We are, as Thérèse shows us in *The Story of a Soul*, brought closer to you through the sufferings we bear and, in that light, we can bear those sufferings with the knowledge that we will come to know your love and mercy ever more through them. Lord Jesus, grant me this wisdom always so I might view my suffering as one more way to know the depths of your love. Amen.

LENTEN ACTION

During your day today, take time to reflect on the suffering you have experienced thus far in your life. Were some of these sufferings physical? Were some emotional or psychological? How did you view those moments of suffering then? Do you view them in a different way now that you have read Thérèse's insights on the possibilities and promises of suffering? She found greater depth in her love for the Lord through her suffering, uniting her anguish to that which Jesus suffered throughout his earthly life, especially the agony he came to experience on Good Friday.

DAY 26

Seeing God in the Face of the Other

A holy nun of our community annoyed me in all that she did; the devil must have had something to do with it, and he it was undoubtedly who made me see in her so many disagreeable points. I did not want to yield to my natural antipathy, for I remembered that charity ought to betray itself in deeds and not exist merely in the feelings, so I set myself to do for this sister all I should do for the one I loved most....

I did not rest satisfied with praying for this Sister, who gave me such occasions for self-mastery, I tried to render her as many services as I could, and when tempted to answer her sharply, I made haste to smile and change the subject....

One day she said to me with a beaming face: "My dear Soeur Thérèse, tell me what attraction you find in me, for whenever we meet, you greet me with such a sweet smile." Ah! What attracted me was Jesus hidden in the depths of her soul—Jesus who maketh sweet even that which is most bitter.

THE STORY OF A SOUL, IX, "THE NIGHT OF THE SOUL"

SCRIPTURE

We have come to know and to believe in the love God has for us. God is love, and whoever remains in love remains in God and God in him. In this is love brought to perfection among us, that we have confidence on the day of judgment because as he is, so are we in this world. There is no fear in love, but perfect love drives out fear because fear has to do with punishment, and so one who fears is not yet perfect in love. We love because he first loved us. If anyone says, "I love God," but hates his brother, he is a liar; for whoever does not love a brother whom he has seen cannot love God whom he has not seen. This is the commandment we have from him: whoever loves God must also love his brother.

1 JOHN 4:16–21

PRAYER

Lord Jesus, you are within every person I encounter in my life, even in those people who irritate me. We are made in your image and, because of this, your image is imprinted on each and every one of us, the people we like and those we do not find pleasant. Lord, give me the grace to see your image in everyone I meet, especially those people who rub me the wrong way. You are in them all, and when I find you there I am amazed I did not see you before. Grace me with the perseverance to find you in all people, Lord, that I may express my love for you through my love toward them. Amen.

LENTEN ACTION

Some day in the coming week, spend ten to fifteen minutes in eucharistic adoration before the Blessed Sacrament. (Many churches have special areas dedicated to this type of worship, and many times available throughout the week during which the area is open for people to come and worship.) During this time you have set aside, make a point of asking the Lord to help you to see his image and presence within those specific people in your life whom you find unpleasant or irritating. Meditate on this matter and offer up any difficulties you may have to the Lord for his grace and guidance.

DAY 27

Trust in His Mercy

*A*fter so many graces, may I not sing with the psalmist that "the Lord is good, that His Mercy endureth for ever" (117:2)? It seems to me that if everyone were to receive such favours, God would be feared by none but loved to excess; that no one would ever commit the least willful fault—and this through love, not fear.

THE STORY OF A SOUL, VIII, "PROFESSION OF SOEUR THÉRÈSE"

SCRIPTURE

I am grateful to him who has strengthened me, Christ Jesus our Lord, because he considered me trustworthy in appointing me to the ministry. I was once a blasphemer and a persecutor and an arrogant man, but I have been mercifully treated because I acted out of ignorance in my unbelief. Indeed, the grace of our Lord has been abundant, along with the faith and love that are in Christ Jesus. This saying is trustworthy and deserves full acceptance: Christ Jesus came into the world to save sinners. Of these I am the foremost. But for that reason I was mercifully treated, so that in me, as the foremost, Christ Jesus might display all his patience as an example for those who would come to believe in him for everlasting life.

1 TIMOTHY 1:12–16

PRAYER

Merciful Father, you know all my shortcomings and all my faults, and in spite of this, perhaps because of this, you show such great mercy and compassion. Let me know your assurance of this mercy and make me confident that my sins and shortcomings bring me closer to you when I bring them to you in humility and repentance. I am but a humble and sinful creature, filled with faults and shortcomings, and you treat me with only mercy and love and forgiveness. Move me beyond fear and move me to repent, dear Father, so that I may experience your mercy all the more. I ask this in the name of your Son, our Lord Jesus Christ. Amen.

LENTEN ACTION

How long has it been since you have known the grace of the sacrament of reconciliation? Perhaps, during the Lenten season, it is time to move beyond any fear you might have and approach the Lord in humility to make a good confession. Make a list of your shortcomings and sins, how you have offended the Lord in sinning against others and harming yourself by distancing yourself from the Lord and his graces. Take these sins to the Lord in confession and allow him to shower his mercy upon you as he desires. He does not want your fear to keep you away from him. Lent is a time of forgiveness. Ask the Lord for his forgiveness, and make it a point to forgive yourself as well.

DAY 28

TUESDAY OF THE FOURTH WEEK OF LENT

God Provides All the Strength We Need

I know your will, dear Mother.* You wish me to carry out, at your side, a work which is both sweet and easy, and this work I shall complete in Heaven. You have said to me, as Our Lord said to St. Peter: "Feed my lambs." I am amazed, for I feel that I am so little. I have entreated you to feed your little lambs yourself and to keep me among them. You have complied in part with my reasonable wish, and have called me their companion, rather than their mistress, telling me nevertheless to lead them through fertile and shady pastures, to point out where the grass is sweetest and best, and warn them against the brilliant but poisonous flowers, which they must never touch except to crush under foot.

How is it, dear Mother, that my youth and inexperience have not frightened you? Are you not afraid that I shall let your lambs stray afar? In acting as you have done, perhaps you remembered that Our Lord is often pleased to give wisdom to little ones.

THE STORY OF A SOUL, IX, "THE NIGHT OF THE SOUL"

* *Saint Thérèse had charge of the novices without being given the title of Novice Mistress.*

SCRIPTURE

Whom else have I in the heavens?
None beside you delights me on earth.
Though my flesh and my heart fail,
God is the rock of my heart, my portion forever.

PSALM 73:25–26

PRAYER

Great and loving God, you have created me for one purpose: to love you, serve you, and praise your holy name all the days of my life. May I love and serve you through my love and service to my brothers and sisters, all of whom were made in your image. May I praise your holy name in everything I do and say, from the church in which I pray and into the streets upon which I serve my brothers and sisters for love of you, who I see in each and every one of their faces. Move me, dear Lord, to offer up every moment of my life to you. From waking in the morning to going to sleep at night, may you fill my day with every opportunity to praise your holy name. Amen.

LENTEN ACTION

During your day today or throughout your day tomorrow, take time to reflect on your words and actions as you speak and as you act. Deliberately consider how God is a part of every word you say and every action you take. (You'll probably go about your speech and movements in a slower manner when you participate in this exercise, but that's fine.) How does thoroughly reflecting on your speech and behavior in this way affect your understanding of God as an integral part of every minute aspect of your life? Do you see how every word, action, and moment is sacred when you praise God and love God in everything you say and do? Consider the "Little Way" of St. Thérèse—do you see now how she embraced her love of and service to God in this very way in everything she did and said throughout her days? Reflect on this and offer a prayer to God.

DAY 29

God Raises Me Up After I Fall

*J*esus watched over His little Spouse and turned even her faults to advantage, for, being checked early in life, they became a means of leading her towards perfection. For instance, as I had great self-love and an innate love of good as well, it was enough to tell me once: "You must not do that," and I never wanted to do it again. Having only good example before my eyes, I naturally wished to follow it, and I see with pleasure in my Mother's letters that as I grew older I began to be a greater comfort.

THE STORY OF A SOUL, I, "EARLIEST MEMORIES"

SCRIPTURE

Thus says the LORD: Cursed is the man who trusts in human beings, who seeks his strength in flesh, whose heart turns away from the LORD. He is like a barren bush in the wasteland that enjoys no change of season, But stands in lava beds in the wilderness, a land, salty and uninhabited. Blessed are those who trust in the LORD; the LORD will be their trust. They are like a tree planted beside the waters that stretches out its roots to the stream: It does not fear heat when it comes, its leaves stay green; In the year of drought it shows no distress, but still produces fruit.

JEREMIAH 17:5–8

PRAYER

Good and holy Lord, you are the source of all love, the heart of all goodness, and the font of grace and healing. You have given me every good thing in my life and, when I am faced with darkness and feelings of insecurity, you are my anchor and my strength. May I never stray from you, oh Lord; keep me on the path of righteousness and attuned to your will. I have known times when I have fallen short of trusting in you, Lord, and I am filled with sadness when I recall those times. But you, dear Lord, draw me close when I dwell on bad times and my trust in you is restored by your grace. May your name be praised by your creation. Amen.

LENTEN ACTION

On an upcoming day, make time to reflect on a moment in your life when your trust in God was at a low point. What was the situation? What part did you play in it? How was your faith affected by this situation? Why was your trust in God absent in this situation? Was it because you were trying to "go it alone" or that you felt God had no place in the situation? Reflect on the situation further: How might the situation have been affected had your trust in God been present? In what ways might God's strength and generosity benefit you should a similar situation arise in the future?

DAY 30

THURSDAY OF THE FOURTH WEEK OF LENT

Motivation to Love

*I*n the Old Law, when God told His people to love their neighbor as themselves, He had not yet come down upon earth; and knowing full well how man loves himself, He could not ask anything greater. But when Our Lord gave His Apostles a New Commandment (see John 13:34)—"His own commandment" (John 15:12)—He was not content with saying: "Thou shalt love thy neighbour as thyself," but would have them love even as He had loved, and as He will love till the end of time.

O my Jesus! Thou does never ask what is impossible; Thou knowest better than I, how frail and imperfect I am, and Thou knowest that I shall never love my Sisters as Thou hast loved them, unless within me Thou lovest them, dear Lord! It is because Thou dost desire to grant me this grace that Thou hast given a New Commandment. Oh how I love it, since I am assured thereby that it is Thy Will to love in me all those Thou dost bid me love!

THE STORY OF A SOUL, IX, "THE NIGHT OF THE SOUL"

SCRIPTURE

Let mutual love continue. Do not neglect hospitality, for through it some have unknowingly entertained angels. Be mindful of prisoners as if sharing their imprisonment, and of the ill-treated as of yourselves, for you also are in the body....Jesus also suffered outside the gate, to consecrate the people by his own blood.... For here we have no lasting city, but we seek the one that is to come. Through him (then) let us continually offer God a sacrifice of praise, that is, the fruit of lips that confess his name. Do not neglect to do good and to share what you have; God is pleased by sacrifices of that kind.

HEBREWS 13:1–3, 12, 14–16

PRAYER

Good and loving God, when I open my heart to you and allow myself to serve as an instrument of your loving grace, my brothers and sisters—those I know and those who are strangers to me—are exposed to and bask in your great love for the men and women you have created and whom you love so dearly and on a personal level. What a tremendous gift you give to me, to show your great love for others through me, your willing servant. Move me, dear Lord, to offer myself ever more in the capacity to open my heart to your presence so that others will know of your great love through me, your humble instrument. Amen.

LENTEN ACTION

During your day today or tomorrow, reflect on your role as an instrument of God, a willing vessel open to sharing the love of God with everyone you meet and allowing God to share his love through you. How does this realization affect your dealings with those you hold dear to your heart? How does this realization affect the way you perceive your relationship with those you hardly know or those who are complete strangers to you? For example, consider your brief encounter with the teller at the bank, the checkout clerk at the grocery store, the letter carrier, or the people you pass on the street and to whom you may or may not make eye contact. How does the fact that God desires to love others through you affect you in these relationships, however small they may be? Pray on this and let God be your guide.

DAY 31

Leaving God to Meet God

*I*n the first place, my soul had for its daily food the bread of spiritual dryness. Then, too, dear Mother, Our Lord allowed you, unconsciously, to treat me very severely. You found fault with me whenever you met me. I remember once I had left a cobweb in the cloister, and you said to me before the whole community: "It is easy to see that our cloisters are swept by a child of fifteen. It is disgraceful! Go and sweep away that cobweb, and be more careful in the future."

One day it occurred to me that you would certainly prefer me to spend my free time in work instead of in prayer, as was my custom; so I plied my needle industriously without even raising my eyes. No one ever knew of this, as I wished to be faithful to Our Lord and do things solely for Him to see.

THE STORY OF A SOUL, X, "THE NEW COMMANDMENT"

SCRIPTURE

Again he entered the synagogue. There was a man there who had a withered hand. They watched him closely to see if he would cure him on the Sabbath so that they might accuse him. He said to the man with the withered hand, "Come up here before us." Then he said to them, "Is it lawful to do good on the Sabbath rather than to do evil, to save life rather than to destroy it?" But they remained silent. Looking around at them with anger and grieved at their hardness of heart, he said to the man, "Stretch out your hand." He stretched it out and his hand was restored.

MARK 3:1–5

PRAYER

Dear Lord, in the mystical body of Christ you are in everyone I see, and I am moved to show you my love through love of my brothers and sisters. Therefore, dear Lord, grant me the wisdom to know when to leave worship for the sake of serving you through service to others. You are in the monstrance, loving God, and you are in the face of those in greatest need. You know this so very well, dear Lord, and I thank you for the example you have shown me. May I continue to be guided by your loving hand in all things, including worship and service. I ask this in your holy name. Amen.

LENTEN ACTION

During this day or the next, take ten to fifteen minutes to reflect and pray on how you've experienced Jesus in the people you've met throughout your life, especially in recent days. Do you view them as an irritation or a nuisance, seeking to be rid of their company as soon as possible? Or do you take the time to engage them and tend to their need for a shoulder on which to cry, an ear to be heard, a voice for advice, or alms for basic needs? One takes considerably less time than the other. Is it worth the investment of your time to engage people and meet them where they are in their life's journey?

DAY 32

SATURDAY OF THE FOURTH WEEK OF LENT

In All Things, Love

*C*harity provided me with the key to my vocation. I understood that since the Church is a body composed of different members, the noblest and most important of all the organs would not be wanting. I knew that the Church has a heart, that this heart burns with love, and that it is love alone that gives life to its members. I knew that if this love were extinguished, the Apostles would no longer preach the Gospel, and the Martyrs would refuse to shed their blood. I understood that love embraces all vocations, that it is all things, and that it reaches out through all the ages, and to the uttermost limits of the earth, because it is eternal.

THE STORY OF A SOUL, XI, "A CANTICLE OF LOVE"

SCRIPTURE

If I speak in human and angelic tongues but do not have love, I am a resounding gong or a clashing cymbal. And if I have the gift of prophecy and comprehend all mysteries and all knowledge; if I have all faith so as to move mountains but do not have love, I am nothing. If I give away everything I own, and if I hand my

*body over so that I may boast but do not have love, I gain noth-
ing. Love is patient, love is kind. It is not jealous, (love) is not
pompous, it is not inflated, it is not rude, it does not seek its own
interests, it is not quick-tempered, it does not brood over injury,
it does not rejoice over wrongdoing but rejoices with the truth.
It bears all things, believes all things, hopes all things, endures
all things. Love never fails. If there are prophecies, they will be
brought to nothing; if tongues, they will cease; if knowledge, it
will be brought to nothing.*

1 CORINTHIANS 13:1–8

PRAYER

Good and loving God, it is love that moves me to act in accordance
with your will; it is through love that I was created; and it is your
love that graces we with every good thing I have. I ask for nothing
more than this: that you love me every day of my life until I join you
in heaven. You have promised your creation this very thing through
your Son, our Lord and Savior, Jesus Christ. May I abide by your
will in everything I think, say, and do. Keep me strong and on the
straight path when I stumble, fill my mind with your wisdom when I
endeavor to speak out on behalf of what is good and right, and fill my
heart with your compassion when I am faced with situations that test
my love and patience. I pray for all of this in your holy name. Amen.

LENTEN ACTION

During your day today or sometime tomorrow, reflect on the words
of Scripture for this day. Take ten to fifteen minutes and read over
these words several times. Consider the meaning of these words as
they apply to your life. In what ways have you experienced love in the
manner described? In what ways have you shown that love to your
family and friends? To the strangers you've encounter throughout
this past week? In what ways does God's love move you to love in the
manner Jesus has modeled for us in the Scriptures? Can you relate
to the difficulties he faced when he encountered people who refused
his love? How do you respond to others when this happens to you?

DAY 33

FIFTH SUNDAY OF LENT

May Merciful Love Be at the Heart of Judgment

One day when I was thinking over the permission we had to talk together so that we might—as our holy constitutions tells us—incite ourselves more ardently to the love of our Divine Spouse, it came home to me sadly that our conversations did not attain the desired end; and I understood that either I must no longer fear to speak out or else I must put an end to what was degenerating into mere worldly talk. I begged our Lord to inspire me with words, kind and convincing....

The next time we met, the poor little Sister saw at once that my manner had changed, and, blushing deeply, she sat down beside me. I pressed her to my heart and told her gently what was in my mind; then I pointed out to her in what true love consists, and proved that in loving her Prioress with such natural affection she was in reality loving herself. I confided to her the sacrifices of this kind which I had been obliged to make at the beginning of my religious life, and before long her tears were mingled with mine. She admitted very humbly that she was in the wrong and that I was right, and, begging me as a favour always to point out her faults, she promised to begin a new life. From this time our love for one another became truly spiritual; in us were fulfilled these words of the Holy Ghost: "A brother that is helped by his brother is like a strong city" (Proverbs 18:19).

THE STORY OF A SOUL, X, "THE NEW COMMANDMENT"

SCRIPTURE

Blessed are the merciful, for they will be shown mercy.

MATTHEW 5:7

On those who waver, have mercy; save others by snatching them out of the fire; on others have mercy with fear, abhorring even the outer garment stained by the flesh.

JUDE 22, 23

PRAYER

Lord, help me when I fall. Raise me up when I am too hard on myself and help me to understand that I am fallible and wholly reliant on your grace and goodness as I go through my life's journey. When I understand my weakness, dear Lord, I better understand the beautiful relationship we share and I am at peace with my standing as a person created by your love. I am humbled by your constant compassion for me. Move me, Lord, to incorporate the mercy I have shown to myself and the mercy I have felt from you into my relationships with others—that I see these people with an eye of love rather than one of judgment. Amen.

LENTEN ACTION

On this day, take time to be kind to yourself, to forgive yourself any burdens of guilt or self-pity that are weighing you down. Say a prayer for yourself and give yourself positive affirmations throughout, thanking God for the wonderful gifts and talents He has given you. Make a list of these gifts and talents and meditate on each one, calling to mind the ways you have used your gifts in acts of love for others and in praise and honor of God. Take time to treat yourself to a quiet walk, time away from your busy schedule—do not hesitate to ask others for help in making this happen!

DAY 34

MONDAY OF THE FIFTH WEEK OF LENT

Give Thanks to the Lord,
for He is Your Hope

At times my soul tires of this over-sweet food, and I long to hear something other than praise; then Our Lord serves me with a nice little salad, well spiced, with plenty of vinegar—oil alone is wanting, and this it is which makes it more to my taste. And the salad is offered to me by the novices at the moment I least expect. God lifts the veil that hides my faults and my dear little Sisters, beholding me as I really am, do not find me altogether agreeable. With charming simplicity, they tell me how I try them and what they dislike in me; in fact, they are as frank as though they were speaking of someone else, for they are aware that I am pleased when they act in this way.

I am more than pleased—I am transported with delight by this splendid banquet set before me. How can anything so contrary to our natural inclinations afford such extraordinary pleasure? Had I not experienced it, I could not have believed it possible.

THE STORY OF A SOUL, X, "THE NEW COMMANDMENT"

SCRIPTURE

For everything created by God is good, and nothing is to be rejected when received with thanksgiving, for it is made holy by the invocation of God in prayer.

1 TIMOTHY 4:4–5

And let the peace of Christ control your hearts, the peace into which you were also called in one body. And be thankful. Let the word of Christ dwell in you richly, as in all wisdom you teach and admonish one another, singing psalms, hymns, and spiritual songs with gratitude in your hearts to God. And whatever you do, in word or in deed, do everything in the name of the Lord Jesus, giving thanks to God the Father through him.

COLOSSIANS 3:15–17

PRAYER

Great and loving God, source of all hope and joy, dwell in me and move my heart to gratitude. May I rely on you and you alone, for you are the one who has given me every good thing I enjoy in my life. From the beautiful days I enjoy to the wonderful people in my life who bring me such joy to the very fact I am alive and able to experience your tremendous love and mercy, I am ever grateful to you for your constant wellspring of generosity. May I always rely on you, dear Lord, and may I give myself to you in everything I do, say, and think—for it is you who made me and it is to you who am called to give of myself completely. Amen.

LENTEN ACTION

During your day today or tomorrow, take a pen and paper and write out a list of everything in your life for which you are grateful. This list can range from the basics of life (food, family, and life itself) to special experiences (sunsets, laughter of children, or music)— recognize everything for which you are grateful. Review your list and reflect on it. Pray on your list and thank God for all that he has given to you. Offer up to God your love and your joy in service to his will. Commit yourself to experiencing God through all aspects of your life experience—from the routine duties you perform to the special people you encounter throughout your day.

DAY 35

TUESDAY OF THE FIFTH WEEK OF LENT

Give of Yourself Without Ceasing

*T*wo years ago, during Lent, a novice came to me smiling and said: "You would never imagine what I dreamt last night—I thought I was with my sister, who is so worldly, and I wanted to withdraw her from all vain things; to this end I explained the words of your hymn: 'They richly lose who love Thee, dearest Lord; Thine are my perfumes, Thine for evermore.' I felt that my words sank deep into her soul, and I was overjoyed. This morning it seems to me that perhaps Our Lord would like me to gain Him this soul. How would it do if I wrote at Easter and described my dream, telling her that Jesus desires to have her for His Spouse?" I answered that she might certainly ask permission.

THE STORY OF A SOUL, X, "THE NEW COMMANDMENT"

SCRIPTURE

Consider this: whoever sows sparingly will also reap sparingly, and whoever sows bountifully will also reap bountifully. Each must do as already determined, without sadness or compulsion, for God loves a cheerful giver. Moreover, God is able to make

77

every grace abundant for you, so that in all things, always hav-
ing all you need, you may have an abundance for every good
work....The one who supplies seed to the sower and bread for
food will supply and multiply your seed and increase the harvest
of your righteousness. You are being enriched in every way for
all generosity, which through us produces thanksgiving to God,
for the administration of this public service is not only supplying
the needs of the holy ones but is also overflowing in many acts
of thanksgiving to God.

2 CORINTHIANS 9:6–8, 10–12

PRAYER

Loving and generous God, you who gives us everything we need,
move my heart to give as you give. Open my heart so that your love
pours through me. Do not allow my selfishness or my vanity to
become an obstacle to what you can give through me. Though I may
be but a little person, small in faith and with little to give, I am a
vessel of your great love, which means my ability to give is limitless.
May I offer no objection to serving as your instrument of love, and
may all who encounter me know your love. I ask this through your
loving Son who allowed the love of his Father in heaven to be known
through the Incarnation. Amen, amen!

LENTEN ACTION

Throughout your day on this day or the next, give of yourself
completely to others by allowing the Lord to love through you. Open
your heart to his will and give all you can to anyone in need. Say
"yes" to anyone who asks for your service, deny no one the good
work and love that comes through you from God. Answer only
"yes" to requests for your assistance and, if you see a need, offer to
help before you can be asked. Allow the Lord to work through you
in every way this day—through your actions, your words, your
willingness to listen, and so on. Understand that through it all it
is the Lord who is loving through you. You are giving yourself as a
vessel for the Lord to love his creation.

DAY 36

Remain Small for the Lord in Joyful Humility

When I say that I am indifferent to praise, I am not speaking, dear Mother, of the love and confidence you show me; on the contrary I am deeply touched thereby, but I feel that I have now nothing to fear, and I can listen to those praises unperturbed, attributing to God all that is good in me. If it please Him to make me appear better than I am, it is nothing to me, He can act as He will. My God, how many ways dost Thou lead souls! We read of Saints who left absolutely nothing at their death, not the least thing by which to remember them, not even a single line of writing; and there are others like our holy Mother, St. Teresa, who have enriched the Church with their sublime teaching, and have not hesitated to reveal "the secrets of the King," (Tobit 12:7) that He may be better known and better loved. Which of these two ways is more pleasing to Our Lord? It seems to me that they are equally so....

You know it has ever been my desire to become a Saint, but I have always felt, in comparing myself with the Saints, that I am as far removed from them as the grain of sand, which the passer-by tramples underfoot, is remote from the mountain whose summit is lost in the clouds.

THE STORY OF A SOUL, IX, "THE NIGHT OF THE SOUL"

SCRIPTURE

Remember how for forty years now the LORD, your God, has directed all your journeying in the desert, so as to test you by affliction and find out whether or not it was your intention to keep his commandments. He therefore let you be afflicted with hunger, and then fed you with manna, a food unknown to you and your fathers, in order to show you that not by bread alone does man live, but by every word that comes forth from the mouth of the LORD....So you must realize that the LORD, your God, disciplines you even as a man disciplines his son. Therefore, keep the commandments of the LORD, your God, by walking in his ways and fearing him....But when you have eaten your fill, you must bless the LORD, your God, for the good country he has given you.

DEUTERONOMY 8:2–3, 5–6, 10

PRAYER

Good and generous Father, you provide me with everything I need. You feed my body and my soul; may I recognize this daily and give thanks for all that you provide me. Keep my eyes set on you, dear Lord, that I might never lose sight of the path you lead me along, that I may always keep in mind that the strength of my spirit relies on you. I am your child, my Father. Keep me on the straight path with your loving hand and know that I seek to please you as a child desires to please her parents. I ask all of this in the name of your Son, our Lord Jesus Christ. Amen.

LENTEN ACTION

Are you poet? Yes or no, try your hand at penning a poem for the Lord. The theme is: "The Lord Is My Guide, My Father, and I Am his Child." Take fifteen minutes to write out your love for the Lord in verse. It can rhyme, but it doesn't have to. It can be long or short. See what you come up with. Perhaps this poem can become a personal prayer for you that you continue to pray even after the Lenten season. Allow the Lord to guide you in your words throughout the process.

DAY 37

The Truly Poor Are Happy

⟨T⟩here is no joy equal to that which is shared by the truly poor in spirit. If they ask with detachment for something necessary, and not only is it refused, but an attempt is made to take away what they already possess, they are following the Master's advice: "If any man will take away thy coat, let him have thy cloak also" (Matthew 5:40). To give up one's cloak is, it seems to me, to renounce every right, and to regard oneself as the servant, the slave, of all. Without a cloak it is easier to walk or run, and so the Master adds: "And whosoever shall force thee to go one mile, go with him other two" (Matthew 5:41).

THE STORY OF A SOUL, IX, "THE NIGHT OF THE SOUL"

SCRIPTURE

Now someone approached him and said, "Teacher, what good must I do to gain eternal life?" He answered him, "Why do you ask me about the good? There is only One who is good. If you wish to enter into life, keep the commandments." He asked him,

"Which ones?" And Jesus replied, "'You shall not kill; you shall not commit adultery; you shall not steal; you shall not bear false witness; honor your father and your mother'; and 'you shall love your neighbor as yourself.'" The young man said to him, "All of these I have observed. What do I still lack?" Jesus said to him, "If you wish to be perfect, go, sell what you have and give to (the) poor, and you will have treasure in heaven. Then come, follow me." When the young man heard this statement, he went away sad, for he had many possessions. Then Jesus said to his disciples, "Amen, I say to you, it will be hard for one who is rich to enter the kingdom of heaven. Again I say to you, it is easier for a camel to pass through the eye of a needle than for one who is rich to enter the kingdom of God." When the disciples heard this, they were greatly astonished and said, "Who then can be saved?" Jesus looked at them and said, "For human beings this is impossible, but for God all things are possible."

MATTHEW 19:16–26

PRAYER

Good and generous God, you give me everything I need. I want for nothing, as you care for me moment to moment. I am left empty when I rely on those things that have nothing to do with you. When I concern myself with power and prestige, when I focus on possessions that have nothing to do with true fulfillment, I am lost at sea without a guiding light. Move me to live poor, dear Lord, in the best and most fulfilling sense of the word. Move me to rely on only your grace and not upon those things that are illusions of security and are but temporary in their standing—power, approval of others, riches, attractiveness, possessions, and pride. Move me to invest my life in love, that is, love for you, love for others, and love for every good thing that brings me closer to you, my good and loving Father. I ask this all in the name of your Son, my Lord and Savior Jesus Christ. Amen.

LENTEN ACTION

During your day today or sometime tomorrow, take ten minutes to reflect on those elements of your life that make you truly happy. Are you filled with joy when you think about the people in your life? Your family and friends? Are you happy when you think about your relationship with Jesus? Now think about your possessions. Do thoughts of these fill you with joy? Most often, thoughts of what we have are unfulfilling and anxiety-inducing, as thoughts of losing our possessions are certain to follow. Spend time today cherishing those elements of your life that fulfill you and bring you joy. Spend time with family and friends, and spend time in prayer fostering your relationship with the Lord.

DAY 38

FRIDAY OF THE FIFTH WEEK OF LENT

How Small, the Treasures of Earth!

*I*f an artist's canvas could but think and speak, surely it would never complain of being touched and re-touched by the brush, nor would it feel envious thereof, knowing that all its beauty is due to the artist alone. So, too, the brush itself could not boast of the masterpiece it had helped to produce, for it must know that an artist is never at a loss; that difficulties do but stimulate him.

THE STORY OF A SOUL, X, "THE NEW COMMANDMENT"

SCRIPTURE

I call heaven and earth today to witness against you: I have set before you life and death, the blessing and the curse. Choose life, then, that you and your descendants may live, by loving the LORD, your God, obeying his voice, and holding fast to him. For that will mean life for you, a long life for you to live on the land which the LORD swore to your ancestors, to Abraham, Isaac, and Jacob, to give to them.

DEUTERONOMY 30:19–20

Then Jesus said to his disciples, "Whoever wishes to come after me must deny himself, take up his cross, and follow me. For whoever wishes to save his life will lose it, but whoever loses his life for my sake will find it. What profit would there be for one to gain the whole world and forfeit his life? Or what can one give in exchange for his life?"

MATTHEW 16:24–26

PRAYER

Lord of heaven and earth, help me to understand the benefits of both of these realms. The earth has much to offer me and many ways by which I can come to know you at ever deeper levels. Make me aware of all paths to you—paths that include prayer, music, food, exercise, the company of friends, the joy of reading and writing, of film and dance. May I come to know you in all things within your sacred creation. What you have created and given me is good, for it has come from you; may I come to know you through every good thing you give. Amen.

LENTEN ACTION

During your day today or tomorrow, explore various ways by which you are brought closer to the Lord through his creation. What good things from God do you find bring you closer to God? What music lifts your spirit to greater heights and deeper reflection on the Lord? Spend time listening to that music. What books—religious or otherwise—bring you in closer contact with the divine? Make time in your day to read parts of these books. What films move you to see the good in God's creation? Take time to view one of these films tonight. Understand that through music and art, food, and exercise, we can come to experience God at a deeper level. God created good things for us to experience on this earth, and these good things can keep our focus on heaven!

DAY 39

In Humility We Are United to Our Lord

I have said Jesus does not wish me to ask again for what is my own. This ought to seem quite easy, for, in reality, nothing is mine. I ought, then, to be glad when an occasion arises which brings home to me the poverty to which I am vowed. I used to think myself completely detached, but since Our Lord's words have become clear, I see that I am indeed very imperfect.

For instance: when starting to paint, if I find the brushes in disorder and a ruler or penknife gone, I feel inclined to lose patience and have to keep a firm hold over myself not to betray my feelings. Of course I may ask for these needful things, and if I do so humbly I am not disobeying Our Lord's command. I am then like the poor who hold out their hands for the necessaries of life, and, if refused, are not surprised, since no one owes them anything.

THE STORY OF A SOUL, IX, "THE NIGHT OF THE SOUL"

SCRIPTURE

If there is any encouragement in Christ, any solace in love, any participation in the Spirit, any compassion and mercy, complete my joy by being of the same mind, with the same love, united in heart, thinking one thing. Do nothing out of selfishness or out of vainglory; rather, humbly regard others as more important than yourselves, each looking out not for his own interests, but (also) everyone for those of others. Have among yourselves the same attitude that is also yours in Christ Jesus, who, though he was in the form of God, did not regard equality with God something to be grasped. Rather, he emptied himself, taking the form of a slave, coming in human likeness; and found human in appearance, he humbled himself, becoming obedient to death, even death on a cross.

PHILIPPIANS 2:1–8

PRAYER

Loving Jesus, you who humbled yourself to become man, who showed us what it is to be truly human and what it means to express one's humanity to the fullest, I come to you today with a simple request: by your unending grace, move my heart to embrace my humanity in the manner you have modeled. May I express myself with love and may I understand that it is through humbling oneself that one unites himself with you—beyond ambition, beyond conceit, and beyond any and all selfishness that prevents one from enjoying the true beauty of the human condition. Create in me, dear Lord, a heart poor in spirit, a heart humble in service and obedient to you. Through this experience of what it is to be truly human, I pray that you and I are united in our shared humanity. Amen.

LENTEN ACTION

During your day today or sometime tomorrow, reflect on what it means to be "poor in spirit," that is, what it means to humble yourself, to serve others in a manner in which you understand yourself to be no better than anyone else. How does this understanding affect your relationship with God, especially as it concerns the Incarnation? How does full reliance on God, without dependence on your own strength—and viewing the needs of others as more important than your own—help you to understand your place in God's creation and your role as a Christian and as a servant to all people? What aspects of your personality make this stance difficult to uphold? In what way—if any—does your pride or self-image affect the perspective of identifying yourself to this degree of humility?

DAY 40

All Members of the Same Body

To pray for sinners delighted me; to pray for Priests, whose souls seemed pure as crystal, that indeed astonished me. But in Italy I realised my vocation, and even so long a journey was a small price to pay for such valuable knowledge. During that month I met with many holy Priests, and yet I saw that even though the sublime dignity of Priesthood raises them higher than the Angels, they are still but weak and imperfect men. And so if holy Priests, whom Our Lord in the Gospel calls the salt of the earth, have need of our prayers, what must we think of the lukewarm? ...Oh, dear Mother, how beautiful is our vocation! We Carmelites are called to preserve "the salt of the earth." We offer our prayers and sacrifices for the apostles of the Lord; we ourselves ought to be their apostles, while they, by word and example, are preaching the Gospel to our brethren. Have we not a glorious mission to fulfill?

THE STORY OF A SOUL, VI, "A PILGRIMAGE TO ROME"

SCRIPTURE

As a body is one though it has many parts, and all the parts of the body, though many, are one body, so also Christ. For in one Spirit we were all baptized into one body, whether Jews or Greeks, slaves or free persons, and we were all given to drink of one Spirit....But as it is, there are many parts, yet one body.... If (one) part suffers, all the parts suffer with it; if one part is honored, all the parts share its joy.

1 CORINTHIANS 12:12–13, 20, 26

PRAYER

Good and generous Father, you grace with me every good thing, every help that I need on my life's journey. Not least among this assistance is your glorious communion of saints, those blessed members of heaven who intervene for me when I call upon them, when I am most in need of your grace. Move me to rely ever more on these loving souls who once shared my own earthly struggles and who overcame death by your loving and guiding hand. May the communion of saints always intercede on my behalf, dear Lord, and may I join their assembly according to your will. Amen.

LENTEN ACTION

If you don't currently incorporate communion with saints into your prayer life (and even if you do), take time this day or the next and research some of the great saints of our Church's history. You can do this online, via a library reference, or through your parish church or rectory. Explore some of the diverse personalities and exciting people the Church upholds as examples by which to model our lives. Write a prayer to a saint who you feel "speaks" to you. In this prayer, ask for this saint's intercession based on the shared earthly experience and struggle he or she shares with you.

DAY 41

MONDAY OF HOLY WEEK

God's Love Moves Us to Pray for Others

*I*f iron and fire were endowed with reason, and the iron could say: "Draw me!" would not that prove its desire to be identified with the fire to the point of sharing its substance? Well, this is precisely my prayer. I asked Jesus to draw me into the Fire of His love, and to unite me so closely to Himself that He may live and act in me. I feel that the more the fire of love consumes my heart, so much the more shall I say: "Draw me!" and the more also will souls who draw near me run swiftly "in the sweet odour of the Beloved."

THE STORY OF A SOUL, XI, "A CANTICLE OF LOVE"

SCRIPTURE

Is anyone among you suffering? He should pray. Is anyone in good spirits? He should sing praise. Is anyone among you sick? He should summon the presbyters of the church, and they should pray over him and anoint (him) with oil in the name of the

Lord, and the prayer of faith will save the sick person, and the Lord will raise him up. If he has committed any sins, he will be forgiven. Therefore, confess your sins to one another and pray for one another, that you may be healed. The fervent prayer of a righteous person is very powerful.

JAMES 5:13–16

PRAYER

Good and loving God, you who care for each of us in a personal and intimate fashion, move me to think of others throughout my day. May I act according to your will when I experience other people in any situation. May others see you in me through everything I do and say. Move me to the full realization that what I do and say affect those around me, especially young adults and children. May I know your way, more and more, each and every day, and may I come to a greater understanding of your love for me by loving others and showing them the love you have for your creation. Through this process, dear Lord, will my soul be brought ever closer to your loving heart. Amen.

LENTEN ACTION

Take time during this day or tomorrow and reflect on the amount of time you spend during the day thinking of and praying for others. Who do you include in your daily prayers? Why do you pray for these specific people? When you are in the company of others, do you make it a point to model God's love for his beloved creatures by listening to and offering to assist your brothers and sisters in need? What kind of example do you set for others, especially young adults and children? In what ways are you brought closer to God when you offer up the needs of others to the Lord's healing grace instead of your needs?

DAY 42

TUESDAY OF HOLY WEEK

Finding God Even in Our Aggravation

For a long time my place at meditation was near a Sister who fidgeted continually, either with her Rosary, or something else; possibly, as I am very quick of hearing, I alone heard her, but I cannot tell you how much it tried me. I should have liked to turn round, and by looking at the offender, make her stop the noise; but in my heart I knew that I ought to bear it tranquilly, both for the love of God and to avoid giving pain. So I kept quiet, but the effort cost me so much that sometimes I was bathed in perspiration, and my meditation consisted merely in suffering with patience. After a time I tried to endure it in peace and joy, at least deep down in my soul, and I strove to take actual pleasure in the disagreeable little noise.

Instead of trying not to hear it, which was impossible, I set myself to listen, as though it had been some delightful music, and my meditation—which was not the "prayer of quiet"—was passed in offering this music to Our Lord.

THE STORY OF A SOUL, X, "THE NEW COMMANDMENT"

SCRIPTURE

One of the scribes, when he came forward and heard them disputing and saw how well he had answered them, asked him, "Which is the first of all the commandments?" Jesus replied, "The first is this: 'Hear, O Israel! The Lord our God is Lord alone! You shall love the Lord your God with all your heart, with all your soul, with all your mind, and with all your strength.' The second is this: 'You shall love your neighbor as yourself.' There is no other commandment greater than these." The scribe said to him, "Well said, teacher. You are right in saying, 'He is One and there is no other than he.' And 'to love him with all your heart, with all your understanding, with all your strength, and to love your neighbor as yourself' is worth more than all burnt offerings and sacrifices." And when Jesus saw that (he) answered with understanding, he said to him, "You are not far from the kingdom of God." And no one dared to ask him any more questions.

MARK 12:28–34

PRAYER

Good and patient God, you know well the struggles we face in our daily lives, those little aggravations that distract us from recognizing you in the person who is annoying us. How you might be aggravated by our own fidgeting and indecisiveness were you not the loving God you are. You see us with nothing but love and those habits that others might find annoying move you to love us all the more. Help me, dear Lord, to see others with those same eyes and to love others, especially those who aggravate us, with that same heart. I ask for this grace today, my generous and loving God, that I might see past the annoyance that aggravates me and view all people with a love that knows no conditions. Amen.

LENTEN ACTION

During your day today or tomorrow, call to mind a person who annoys and aggravates you in some way, ideally a person you will see in the not-too-distant future. Reflect on the habit or behavioral tendency this person exhibits that gets under your skin. Why does this behavior aggravate you the way it does? Does it seem to aggravate others in a similar fashion? How do you currently cope with this aggravation? In what ways might you improve this coping strategy? How does this aggravation appear to you when Jesus is brought into the situation? Are you able to see this person with the eyes of Jesus? Pray on this. The next time you are in the company of the person who annoys you, consider how you might affect his or her behavior by conversing and listening with a heart intent on loving the person—annoying habits and all!

DAY 43

There Is No Vanity in the "Last Place"

On this earth, it is rare indeed to find souls who do not measure God's Omnipotence by their own narrow thoughts. The world is always ready to admit exceptions everywhere here below. God alone is denied this liberty. It has long been the custom among men to reckon experience by age, for in his youth the holy King David sang to His Lord: "I am young and despised," (Psalm 119:141) but in the same Psalm he says: "I have had understanding above old men, because I have sought Thy commandments, Thy word is a lamp to my feet, and a light to my paths; I have sworn, and I am determined, to keep the judgments of Thy Justice" (Psalm 119:100,105–106).

And you did not even consider it imprudent to assure me one day, that the Divine Master had enlightened my soul and given me the experience of years. I am too little now to be guilty of vanity; I am likewise too little to endeavour to prove my humility by fine-sounding words. I prefer to own in all simplicity that "He that is mighty hath done great things to me" (Luke 1:49).

THE STORY OF A SOUL, IX, "THE NIGHT OF THE SOUL"

SCRIPTURE

He told a parable to those who had been invited, noticing how they were choosing the places of honor at the table. "When you are invited by someone to a wedding banquet, do not recline at table in the place of honor. A more distinguished guest than you may have been invited by him, and the host who invited both of you may approach you and say, 'Give your place to this man,' and then you would proceed with embarrassment to take the lowest place. Rather, when you are invited, go and take the lowest place so that when the host comes to you he may say, 'My friend, move up to a higher position.' Then you will enjoy the esteem of your companions at the table. For everyone who exalts himself will be humbled, but the one who humbles himself will be exalted."

LUKE 14:7–11

PRAYER

Loving Jesus, you humbled yourself through the Incarnation, becoming human so that you might experience the life of your most beloved creation. You made sacred every aspect of the human experience throughout your life, defeating death through your crucifixion and winning for all the treasure of eternal life in heaven with you. You chose to enter this world as the member of a poor and humble family, not in royal splendor. Through this fact, you showed us that to be truly human, one must only love. Riches play no part, and neither does social standing. Thank you for showing us that unity with God can be brought forth by a humble heart, a heart dedicated only to love and not to the distractions of wealth and worldly success. Amen.

LENTEN ACTION

During your day today or tomorrow, take ten to fifteen minutes to reflect on the concept of humility. In what ways do you humble yourself? When do you humble yourself, and in what ways does it deepen your relationship with God? In situations when you humble yourself—or are humbled without making the effort—do you gain a greater appreciation for the humility Jesus experienced during his earthly life? In what ways can you further humble yourself during this Lenten season? Try to incorporate these "humility exercises" throughout the remaining days of Lent and observe how you feel during these experiences and in what ways your relationship with Jesus is deepened.

DAY 44

HOLY THURSDAY

Temptation

$\mathcal{H}$ow can a heart given up to human affections be closely united to God? It seems to me that it is impossible. I have seen so many souls, allured by this false light, fly right into it like poor moths, and burn their wings, and then return, wounded, to Our Lord, the Divine fire which burns and does not consume. I know well Our Lord saw that I was too weak to be exposed to temptation, for, without doubt, had the deceitful light of created love dazzled my eyes, I should have been entirely consumed. Where strong souls find joy and practice detachment faithfully, I only found bitterness. No merit, then, is due to me for not having given up to these frailties, since I was only preserved from them by the Mercy of God.

THE STORY OF A SOUL, IV, "FIRST COMMUNION AND CONFIRMATION"

SCRIPTURE

Then Jesus came with them to a place called Gethsemane, and he said to his disciples, "Sit here while I go over there and pray." He took along Peter and the two sons of Zebedee, and began to feel sorrow and distress. Then he said to them, "My soul is sorrowful even to death. Remain here and keep watch with me." He advanced a little and fell prostrate in prayer, saying, "My Father, if it is possible, let this cup pass from me; yet, not as I will, but as you will." When he returned to his disciples he found them asleep. He said to Peter, "So you could not keep watch with me for one hour? Watch and pray that you may not undergo the test. The spirit is willing, but the flesh is weak."

MATTHEW 26:36–41

PRAYER

Loving and caring Jesus, protect me from the temptations that confront me throughout my day and keep me safe from sin. When I do stumble, Lord, bring me to my feet and hold me even closer. Dear Jesus, you know well the temptations that cross our paths throughout our lives on this earth. Keep me steadfast in prayer and focused on God's will, the characteristics you exemplified during your agony in the Garden of Gethsemane. Jesus, you are by my side daily and throughout the night, never wavering, my constant support in the face of evil. Keep me on the righteous path, close to you, and never let me go. Amen.

LENTEN ACTION

Take a few moments to call to mind some of the "Gethsemane" moments in your life. These may or may not have been life-or-death situations. Consider the following questions as you look back in time: How did you prepare for them (if you could)? Who did you turn to in anticipation of something difficult or terrible coming into your life? Did you receive the support of family or friends? Did you feel like there was no one there to help you or there wasn't anything anyone could do to help? Did you try to go it alone? Did you turn to God during this time? If so, try to recollect your prayer. What elements comprised this prayer? Did you feel in touch with God? What type of response did you receive?

DAY 45

Love Your Enemies

*A*nd it is the Lord, it is Jesus, Who is my judge. Therefore I will try always to think leniently of others, that He may judge me leniently, or rather not at all, since He says: "Judge not, and ye shall not be judged"[23].

But returning to the Holy Gospel where Our Lord explains to me clearly in what His New Commandment consists, I read in St. Matthew: "You have heard that it hath been said, Thou shalt love thy neighbour, and hate thy enemy: but I say unto you, Love your enemies, and pray for them that persecute you"[24].

THE STORY OF A SOUL, IX, "THE NIGHT OF THE SOUL"

SCRIPTURE

But to you who hear I say, love your enemies, do good to those who hate you, bless those who curse you, pray for those who mistreat you. To the person who strikes you on one cheek, offer the other one as well, and from the person who takes your cloak,

do not withhold even your tunic. Give to everyone who asks of
you, and from the one who takes what is yours do not demand
it back. Do to others as you would have them do to you.

LUKE 6:27–31

PRAYER

Merciful and loving God, you love all people you have created, regardless of how cruel they may seem to the eye of the observer. Your love falls like rain from the sky, nourishing both the beautiful flowers and the thorny bush; your love is given without prejudice and without condition. May I, by your grace, love in an unconditional manner and give myself completely in service and love to all types of people, regardless of how others—or I—might feel about them. Move me, Lord, to embrace in my heart those very people who have hurt me in the past. Though I protect myself from their wickedness, dear Lord, I open my heart to let you love them through me. In your name, and with the power of the Holy Spirit, I ask that you guide me in all things, especially during trying and difficult times. Amen.

LENTEN ACTION

During your day today or tomorrow, set aside fifteen to twenty minutes for reflection. Reflect on the topic of "loving your enemy." What does it mean to love your enemy? Does it mean allowing yourself to be hurt time and again by a person with seemingly cruel intentions? Does it mean praying for this person from afar, distancing yourself from him/her, and not allowing the person to poison your life? Does "loving your enemy" mean wishing that person well but, in fact, harboring tremendous feelings of anger and dread within you? How does one truly love an enemy? What does it mean to love an enemy in a way that protects you, expresses love for the other, and allows you to be at peace with yourself and that person and free of toxic emotions associated with this person?

DAY 46

God Is My Protection, He Consoles Me

My dear Mother died on August 28, 1877, in her forty-sixth year. The day after her death, my Father took me in his arms and said: "Come and kiss your dear Mother for the last time." Without saying a word I put my lips to her icy forehead. I do not remember having cried much, and I did not talk to anyone of all that filled my heart; I looked and listened in silence, and I saw many things they would have hidden from me. Once I found myself close to the coffin in the passage. I stood looking at it for a long time; I had never seen one before, but I knew what it was. I was so small that I had to lift up my head to see its whole length, and it seemed to me very big and very sad.

THE STORY OF A SOUL, II, "A CATHOLIC HOUSEHOLD"

SCRIPTURE

My God, my rock of refuge, my shield, my saving horn, my stronghold!

PSALM 18:3

At dusk weeping comes for the night; but at dawn there is rejoicing.

PSALM 30:6

The salvation of the righteous is from the LORD, their refuge in a time of distress.

PSALM 37:39

God is our refuge and our strength, an ever-present help in distress. Thus we do not fear, though earth be shaken and mountains quake to the depths of the sea.

PSALM 46:2–3

PRAYER

Kind and comforting Lord, you are beside me through all difficulties, whenever obstacles come before me, and whenever I am visited by grief and sadness. Simply knowing that you are with me, Lord, is all the comfort I need, but I thank you for all others comforts you provide me during my times of sadness. I thank you for the friends and family I love and on whom I rely, as they express your love and concern for me in a tangible manner. I thank you for solitude and time to reflect when I am grieving, for this time allows me to invite you deeper into my life and to share my grieving, allowing me to understand how I can grow ever closer to you during this difficulty. Move me, Lord, to know and love you to the greatest depths my suffering, loneliness, and sorrow can provide. Amen.

LENTEN ACTION

During your day today, go to a place in your home or wherever you are so you can be in complete silence. For fifteen to twenty minutes, reflect on the sorrow that the apostles and Mary, the Mother of our Lord, experienced on Holy Saturday. Consider the grief felt by these people—friends of the Lord, Jesus' Mother—after they witnessed his brutal murder. Put yourself in their place and consider the grief you have felt in your own life. How much did sorrow consume you during your suffering? Were friends and family able to console you? Did you feel God at work through anyone or anything during your time of sadness and grief? Was your relationship with God strengthened during this period of grief or was it damaged? Pray on all of this.

PART II

~~~~~~

READINGS *for* EASTER

DAY 47

EASTER

Rejoice! The Lord Is Risen

Many were the graces I asked. I felt myself truly a queen and took advantage of my title to obtain every favour from the King for His ungrateful subjects. No one was forgotten. I wished that every sinner on earth might be converted; that on that day Purgatory should set its captives free; and I bore upon my heart this letter containing what I desired for myself:

O Jesus, my Divine Spouse, grant that my baptismal robe may never be sullied. Take me from this world rather than let me stain my soul by committing the least willful fault. May I never seek or find aught but Thee alone! May all creatures be nothing to me and I nothing to them! May no earthly thing disturb my peace!

THE STORY OF A SOUL, VIII, "PROFESSION OF SOEUR THÉRÈSE"

SCRIPTURE

After the sabbath, as the first day of the week was dawning, Mary Magdalene and the other Mary came to see the tomb. And behold, there was a great earthquake; for an angel of the Lord descended from heaven, approached, rolled back the stone, and sat upon it. His appearance was like lightning and his clothing was white as snow. The guards were shaken with fear of him and became like dead men. Then the angel said to the women in reply, "Do not be afraid! I know that you are seeking Jesus the crucified. He is not here, for he has been raised just as he said. Come and see the place where he lay. Then go quickly and tell his disciples, 'He has been raised from the dead, and he is going before you to Galilee; there you will see him.' Behold, I have told you." Then they went away quickly from the tomb, fearful yet overjoyed, and ran to announce this to his disciples. And behold, Jesus met them on their way and greeted them. They approached, embraced his feet, and did him homage. Then Jesus said to them, "Do not be afraid. Go tell my brothers to go to Galilee, and there they will see me."

MATTHEW 28:1–10

PRAYER

Oh, glorious Lord, I thank you for this day, this magnificent day on which you have defeated death and, in doing so, opened the gates of heaven to your beloved creatures, man and woman. I am overcome, good and great God, with gratitude and joy for this blessed day. The hope that you have given me in winning this victory for humankind, is a joy beyond belief. To know that, by your grace, I will be with you in heaven when I depart this earth is to know the greatest love of all. And it is all possible because of you, dear Lord; by your love and grace is this possible, and for this and all that you do in every aspect of my life, I thank you and praise your holy name, now and forever. Amen.

EASTER ACTION

During your day today, keep in mind everything for which you are grateful. From family and friends to good health (your own and others, if applicable) and good food, thank the Lord and praise his name in everything you do and say. Keep in mind your gratitude for God and generosity throughout this day as you experience every person you engage, participate in each activity you do (from setting the table to mashing the potatoes), and in every breath you draw. Remember the Little Way, that is, experiencing the divine in every moment, in everything you say and do. All is given in love of God, no matter how small or routine. This sets a person's eyes on God in every moment, allowing time and space only for God.

DAY 48

Committed to Sincere Love

*H*ow many souls might attain to great sanctity if only they were directed aright from the first! I know God has no need of anyone to help Him in His work of sanctification, but as He allows a clever gardener to cultivate rare and delicate plants, giving him the skill to accomplish it, while reserving to Himself the right of making them grow, so does He wish to be helped in the cultivation of souls.

....This reminds me that I used to have among my birds a canary which sang beautifully, and also a little linnet taken from the nest, of which I was very fond. This poor little prisoner, deprived of the teaching it should have received from its parents, and hearing the joyous trills of the canary from morning to night, tried hard to imitate them. A difficult task indeed for a linnet! It was delightful to follow the efforts of the poor little thing; his sweet voice found great difficulty in accommodating itself to the vibrant notes of his master, but he succeeded in time, and, to my great surprise, his song became exactly like the song of the canary.

THE STORY OF A SOUL, V, "VOCATION OF THÉRÈSE"

SCRIPTURE

The aim of this instruction is love from a pure heart, a good conscience, and a sincere faith. Some people have deviated from these and turned to meaningless talk, wanting to be teachers of the law, but without understanding either what they are saying or what they assert with such assurance.

1 TIMOTHY 1:5–7

Let love be sincere; hate what is evil, hold on to what is good; love one another with mutual affection; anticipate one another in showing honor. Do not grow slack in zeal, be fervent in spirit, serve the Lord. Rejoice in hope, endure in affliction, persevere in prayer. Contribute to the needs of the holy ones, exercise hospitality.

ROMANS 12:9–13

PRAYER

Good and generous Father, God of Love, pour out your love for the world through me, your willing vessel, your instrument. I am here to serve your will without judgment, without bias. Guide me, lead me to those people who desire your love, to those people who need to know your love as they struggle with any and all difficulties they are experiencing at this time. Do not allow me to become distracted by any negative feelings as to who deserves your love and who does not—help me to understand that everyone deserves your love, regardless of my opinion of who they are and what they have done. Join my will with your own so that I might share your love and spread your good news to the everyone in my corner of the world. Amen.

EASTER ACTION

Spend time this day or tomorrow with someone who irritates you or who has irritated you in the past. Give the person your time and attention during the minutes you share, knowing that it is God's abiding and generous love you bring. Notice how your relationship with this person is transformed when you view him or her with eyes of our loving Father. Understand that the only thing that has kept you from loving this person is your judgment. Pray for this person—and for yourself—before and after you share part of your day together.

DAY 49

EASTER TUESDAY

Jesus' Peace Never Leaves Us

ear Mother, I feel that I have expressed myself with more than usual confusion, and I do not know what you can find to interest you in these rambling pages, but I am not aiming at a literary masterpiece, and if I weary you by this discourse on charity, it will at least prove your child's good will. I must confess I am far from living up to my ideal, and yet the very desire to do so gives me a feeling of peace. If I fall into some fault, I arise again at once—and for some months now I have not even had to struggle. I have been able to say with our holy Father, St. John of the Cross: "My house is entirely at peace," and I attribute this interior peace to a victory I gained over myself. Since that victory, the hosts of Heaven have hastened to my aid, for they will not allow me to be wounded, now that I have fought so valiantly.

THE STORY OF A SOUL, IX, "THE NIGHT OF THE SOUL"

SCRIPTURE

Many are the sorrows of the wicked, but love surrounds those who trust in the LORD. Be glad in the LORD and rejoice, you just; exult, all you upright of heart.

PSALM 32:10–11

PRAYER

Steadfast and loving Father, you draw me near when I am in my greatest need. It is you who nourishes me in every way, throughout my days and years. When my life is troubled, dear Father, and beset by gusts of wind that seek to destroy my small boat, help me to understand that the difficulties I encounter on my journey only bring me closer to you when I put my trust and faith completely in you. Move me, Lord, to view my daily troubles as an avenue to greater love and deeper relationship with you, my Father in heaven. I ask this through your Son, and our Lord, Jesus Christ. Amen.

EASTER ACTION

During your day today or tomorrow, take a moment to reflect on the recent difficulties you have experienced in your life. Focus on one or two of these situations and consider how each one brought you—or had the potential to bring you—closer to God. Did the situation seem devoid of the divine as you experienced it? That is common. It can be difficult to be centered and focused on the Lord during times of great difficulty. But after such a situation passes, can you see how the struggle you faced brought you closer to the Lord? Consider praying on this matter—focusing on such a situation—for five minutes.

DAY 50

Love Alone Is Enough

*H*ow shall I show my love, since love proves itself by deeds? Well! The little child will strew flowers, she will embrace the Divine Throne with their fragrance, she will sing Love's Canticle in silvery tones. Yes, my Beloved, it is thus my short life shall be spent in Thy sight. The only way I have of proving my love is to strew flowers before Thee—that is to say, I will let no tiny sacrifice pass, no look, no word. I wish to profit by the smallest actions and to do them for Love. I wish to suffer for Love's sake and for Love's sake even to rejoice: thus shall I strew flowers. Not one shall I find without scattering its petals before Thee...and I will sing...I will sing always, even if my roses must be gathered from amidst thorns; and the longer and sharper the thorns, the sweeter shall be my song.

But of what avail to Thee, my Jesus, are my flowers and my songs? I know it well: this fragrant shower, these delicate petals of little price, these songs of love from a poor little heart like mine, will nevertheless be pleasing unto Thee. Trifles they are, but Thou wilt smile on them.

THE STORY OF A SOUL, XI, "A CANTICLE OF LOVE"

SCRIPTURE

...Jesus said, "I give praise to you, Father, Lord of heaven and earth, for although you have hidden these things from the wise and the learned you have revealed them to the childlike. Yes, Father, such has been your gracious will. All things have been handed over to me by my Father. No one knows the Son except the Father, and no one knows the Father except the Son and anyone to whom the Son wishes to reveal him.

"Come to me, all you who labor and are burdened, and I will give you rest.

MATTHEW 11:25–28

PRAYER

Lord God, keep your message of love in my heart and do not let me stray from you. Keep me childlike in my surrender to you and do not allow the cynicism of the world to corrupt the purity you have instilled in my heart. When I burden myself with those matters that do not contribute to my happiness or well-being, remind me that love alone is enough. When I lose my way and allow distraction and worry to interfere with my attention to you, call me to a greater depth of trust in you. Move me to surrender my doubts and worries, fears and selfishness to your loving hands. When I am with you, dear Lord, I am unburdened and I know that love alone is enough. Amen.

EASTER ACTION

Call a friend you haven't spoken to in a long time. Block out distractions and give your time completely to this person and listen with your whole heart. Tell him or her that you want to spend time conversing for thirty to forty-five minutes. Spend this time listening and be encouraging. That way, your friend will feel appreciated and special.

DAY 51

God Loves All.
We Are Called to Do the Same

*Y*es, I know when I show charity to others, it is simply Jesus acting in me, and the more closely I am united to Him, the more dearly I love my Sisters. If I wish to increase this love in my heart, and the devil tries to bring before me the defects of a Sister, I hasten to look for her virtues, her good motives; I call to mind that though I may have seen her fall once, no doubt she has gained many victories over herself, which in her humility she conceals. It is even possible that what seems to me a fault may very likely, on account of her good intention, be an act of virtue. I have no difficulty in persuading myself of this, because I have had the same experience.

THE STORY OF A SOUL, IX, "THE NIGHT OF THE SOUL"

SCRIPTURE

For God so loved the world that he gave his only Son, so that everyone who believes in him might not perish but might have eternal life. For God did not send his Son into the world to condemn the world, but that the world might be saved through him.

JOHN 3:16–17

PRAYER

Good and loving God, you have created each of us by your love. You have loved us into being and see only value in us. I am blinded, dear Lord, by my own prejudice and shortsightedness when I evaluate others, determining their worth in a self-important manner, never taking into account the basic fact that it is not my estimation of people that gives them value or allows that they are capable of being loved. Their worth is based solely on this: They are loved by you and, therefore, worthy of my love. Move me to see with your eyes, loving Father, and view all your children with your eyes of unfailing love. I ask this in the name of your Son, our Lord Jesus Christ. Amen.

EASTER ACTION

During your day today, tomorrow, and for all days to come, give others the benefit of the doubt in love in all your dealings. God loves people deeply because he has loved them into being. We often cannot readily identify a person's loveliness due to our own lack of understanding as human beings. Obviously, our Lord Jesus knows there is much to love in others. That being the case, the onus is on us to discover that fact for ourselves or, failing that, to understand that others are capable of being loved by the simple reason that they're loved by God. When you are with people you find disagreeable, include them in your prayer for that day and ask God to help you see them with God's eyes of love.

DAY 52

EASTER FRIDAY

Mary Our Mother, Our Blessed Intercessor

On the morning of September 8, a wave of peace flooded my soul, and, in "that peace which surpasseth all understanding" (Philippians 4:7), I pronounced my holy vows.

Grant that I may fulfill my engagements in all their perfection; that no one may think of me; that I may be trodden under foot, forgotten, as a little grain of sand. I offer myself to Thee, O my Beloved, that Thou mayest ever perfectly accomplish in me Thy Holy Will, without let or hindrance from creatures.

When at the close of this glorious day I laid my crown of roses, according to custom, at Our Lady's feet, it was without regret.

It was the Nativity of Mary. What a beautiful feast on which to become the Spouse of Jesus! It was the little newborn Holy Virgin who presented her little Flower to the little Jesus. That day everything was little except the graces I received—except my peace and joy in gazing upon the beautiful starlit sky at night, and in thinking that soon I should fly away to Heaven and be united to my Divine Spouse amid eternal bliss.

THE STORY OF A SOUL, VIII, "PROFESSION OF SOEUR THÉRÈSE"

SCRIPTURE

In the sixth month, the angel Gabriel was sent from God to a town of Galilee called Nazareth, to a virgin betrothed to a man named Joseph, of the house of David, and the virgin's name was Mary. And coming to her, he said, "Hail, favored one! The Lord is with you."

LUKE 1:26–28

When the wine ran short, the mother of Jesus said to him, "They have no wine." (And) Jesus said to her, "Woman, how does your concern affect me? My hour has not yet come." His mother said to the servers, "Do whatever he tells you."

JOHN 2:3–5

PRAYER

Holy Mary, Mother of God, I come to you this day to thank you for your willingness to accept God's love in the manner that you did, as a vessel for our Lord and Savior, Jesus Christ. I come also to seek your help, to ask that you intercede on my behalf. Your Son cannot deny you, dear Mary, for your will is united with his. I ask that you recommend me to your Son, that you ask that his grace be showered upon me in my time of need, when I am tired and near feeling without hope. Speak on my behalf, Blessed Virgin. I call on your assistance and guidance to a deeper relationship with your Son and my Lord Jesus. Amen.

EASTER ACTION

During your day today or tomorrow, make it a point to say "yes" to God throughout your day. Meet every person you meet and every situation you encounter with a "yes"—accepting God's presence and God's will for you in the company of that person. How do you view people and situations when you are in the "yes mode" with God? Does it change your usual behavior to view people and situations with the eyes of Jesus and the will of God? Reflect on your "yes" day during an evening prayer.

DAY 53

Easter Saturday

To Contemplate God's Beauty

*A*bout eight o'clock, Papa would come to fetch me. I remember that I used to look up at the stars with inexpressible delight. Orion's belt fascinated me especially, for I saw in it a likeness to the letter "T." "Look, Papa," I would cry, "my name is written in Heaven!" Then, not wishing to see this dull earth any longer, I asked him to lead me, and with my head thrown back, I gazed unwearied at the starry skies.

THE STORY OF A SOUL, II, "A CATHOLIC HOUSEHOLD"

SCRIPTURE

After their audience with the king [the Magi] set out. And behold, the star that they had seen at its rising preceded them, until it came and stopped over the place where the child was. They were overjoyed at seeing the star, and on entering the house they saw the child with Mary his mother. They prostrated themselves and did him homage. Then they opened their treasures and offered him gifts of gold, frankincense, and myrrh.

MATTHEW 2:9–11

PRAYER

Lord of hope, quiet my heart that I might keep my attention on those good and permanent things that lead me to you. Like the star above the stable in Bethlehem where the Magi found our newborn Savior, may I be aware of the landmarks in my life that point the direction to you. May I see your face in another, may I witness your glory in all your glorious creation, and may I proclaim your goodness in every little thing I do and say. Amen.

EASTER ACTION

Spend this evening with family and friends. Realize the treasure you've been given by the Lord and cherish every moment you share with the ones you love. Give your complete attention to the ones you love and open your heart to them in gratitude for the gift they are from the Lord. Tell them that you are a gift to them from the Lord and that all can come to know God's great love through the love and caring of his instruments, his beloved children.

DAY 54

SECOND SUNDAY OF EASTER

A Vocation of Love

Then, beside myself with joy, I cried out: "O Jesus, my Love, at last I have found my vocation. My vocation is love! Yes, I have found my place in the bosom of the Church, and this place, O my God, Thou hast Thyself given to me: in the heart of the Church, my Mother, I will be Love! Thus I shall be all things: thus will my dream be realized."

Why do I say I am beside myself with joy? This does not convey my thought. Rather is it peace which has become my portion—the calm peace of the sailor when he catches sight of the beacon which lights him to port. O luminous Beacon of Love! I know how to come even unto Thee, I have found the means of borrowing Thy Fires.

I am but a weak and helpless child, yet it is my very weakness which makes me dare to offer myself, O Jesus, as victim to Thy Love.

THE STORY OF A SOUL, XI, "A CANTICLE OF LOVE"

SCRIPTURE

Love never fails. If there are prophecies, they will be brought to nothing; if tongues, they will cease; if knowledge, it will be brought to nothing. For we know partially and we prophesy partially, but when the perfect comes, the partial will pass away. When I was a child, I used to talk as a child, think as a child, reason as a child; when I became a man, I put aside childish things. At present we see indistinctly, as in a mirror, but then face to face. At present I know partially; then I shall know fully, as I am fully known. So faith, hope, love remain, these three; but the greatest of these is love.

1 CORINTHIANS 13:8–13

PRAYER

Oh, my loving Father in heaven, thank you, thank you, thank you for love, the greatest vocation of all. Move me and guide me to love your creation and all the goodness within. May I share your love with my brothers and sisters all the days of my life and strengthen your great Church on this earth. May I pursue love in all things and in everything I do; may I respond with love in the face of anger and hatred; and may I follow love at your side both in earth and in heaven. Amen.

EASTER ACTION

On this day, find a way to share your love with people you know. Perhaps a phone call, a letter, or an email will convey your love for the people in your life. Send them the beautiful scriptural passage from 1 Corinthians. Your thoughtfulness and love will make someone's day, perhaps bringing that person closer to God. Your thoughtfulness and love will make your own day, bringing you closer to God. May you always view the world with love, may you commit yourself to this greatest of all vocations, and may the Lord our God keep you in the palm of his hand.

Other titles in the
Lent and Easter Wisdom series:

Lent and Easter Wisdom
From Fulton J. Sheen

Lent and Easter Wisdom
From Thomas Merton

Lent and Easter Wisdom
From Henri J. M. Nouwen

Lent and Easter Wisdom
From Pope John Paul II

Lent and Easter Wisdom
From G. K. Chesterton

Lent and Easter Wisdom
From St. Ignatius of Loyola

Lent and Easter Wisdom
From St. Benedict

Lent and Easter Wisdom
From St. Alphonsus

Lent and Easter Wisdom
From St. Vincent de Paul

Lent and Easter Wisdom
From St. Augustine

CPSIA information can be obtained
at www.ICGtesting.com
Printed in the USA
FFOW05n1433130115

9 780764 821738